## Table of Contents

# Introduction

On August 17, 2009 an unsuspecting Russian worker began his shift at an obscure hydroelectric dam in central Russia. Without warning, a powerful, multi-ton turbine began to spin, fighting itself as it attempted to defeat its own restraining devices. More specifically, Turbine #2 of the Sayano–Shushenskaya hydroelectric power station, while down for repairs, received the impossible order, via a computer command, to restart itself. The turbine attempted to comply, and so doing, self-destructed and flew fifty feet into the air. What the Russian worker thought as he witnessed one of the first destructive cyber attacks is unknown, as he was killed in the resultant explosion. This attack caused flooding and destruction that killed seventy-five people and caused over one billion dollars in damage. The action was traced to computer instructions emailed from over 500 kilometers away.[1] While many unclassified media sources have described this event as an accident, at least one source has speculated this was a possible network attack.[2] To this day, attribution as to the cause is unclear. What is clear is that an electronic message was sent through the internet, commanding the turbine to restart itself and commit a type of mechanical suicide that achieved lethal effects, killing the Russian mechanic and a number of other people.

Far more famously, on June 17, 2010 a computer virus later named "Stuxnet" attacked the Natanz Nuclear Enrichment Plant in Iran. Computer malware infected tens of thousands of systems, searching for the specific computers used to control automated centrifuges in nuclear plants. They then took over the Iranian code, commanding the system to rapidly accelerate and

---

[1] Robert Johnson, "New Cyber Attacks Will Target Power Grids And Major Public Works," *Business Insider*, (March 10, 2012), under "data theft turbine cyber warfare," http://articles.businessinsider.com/2011-09-14/news/30153012_1_data-theft-turbine-cyber-warfare (accessed February 2, 2012).

[2] Robert E. Schmidle, USMC, Deputy Commander USCYBERCOM "USMC Cyberspace Update," (presentation at meeting of the AFCEA Quantico-Potomac Chapter, Quantico, VA, March 31, 2011).

decelerate the centrifuge spin rate. Again, computer viruses had infected a machine, or in this case hundreds of machines, commanding them to perform impossible tasks until they destroyed themselves. Strategic level national assets were destroyed, or more accurately, commanded to destroy themselves, through cyber attack. By conducting lethal and kinetic strikes, cyber attacks had crossed a new threshold in warfare.[3]

A cyber attack in these instances is represented by a computer virus, or malware, that is sent through the internet to infect or disable a computer. In the past, such viruses could be used to infect a computer, steal information, or break through protective firewalls to extract valuable intelligence. Previously, these cyber attacks gave the impression of a sort of benign, physically harmless threat. Modern cyber attacks can target the computers that control heavy machinery, nuclear power, aviation—the sorts of machines that are most efficiently controlled by computers, but if deliberately mishandled, can result in physical, kinetic effects. Such activities may share different means, but the ends are identical to the lethal strike of conventional high explosive munitions. In the case of Sayano–Shushenskaya, an electronic command was more lethal than many of the large scale bombings of World War II.[4]

The question that arises is, what should the US Department of Defense, specifically US Cyber Command, do about this? This monograph's thesis will rest on the assumption, rarely proven wrong, that in the cyber environment the offense is generally more powerful than defense, and like the bombers of the past, and the megabyte will always get through. Defensive strategies

---

[3] Kim Zetter, "How Digital Detectives Deciphered Stuxnet," *Wired*, (July 11, 2011) under "Stuxnet" http://www.wired.com/threatlevel/2011/07/how-digital-detectives-deciphered-stuxnet/2/ (accessed December 27, 2011).

[4] This was derived by comparing the damage from the Sayano–Shushenskaya as described Alexander Boyko and Sergey Popov "Investigating the Sayano-Shushenskaya Hydro Power Plant Disaster," *Power Magazine*, (December 1, 2010), http://www.powermag.com/issues/features/Investigating-the-Sayano-Shushenskaya-Hydro-Power-Plant-Disaster_3229.html (accessed April 3, 2012), with the damage assessments for Operation Chastise, the World War 2 British campaign against Nazi dams found in John Sweetman, David Coward and Gary Johnstone, *The Dambusters* (London: Time Warner Books, 2003), 169-173.

are less cost effective and not a valid deterrent compared to the alternative of offense, and potential rivals of the United States have outgained us in this area and are moving forward. **The thesis of this paper is that the Joint Cyber Command is undermanned, under resourced, and needs to establish its own educational, personnel, and doctrinal areas of expertise to create the specialized forces needed to succeed in the newest domain of warfare.** The United States is behind, falling further behind, and requires a doctrinal base to set a compass to answer these difficult questions and solve complex, wicked problems involving cyber warfare. At a minimum, a doctrinal and educational center for excellence is needed to pose and answer such questions.

The future strategic and operational environment favors the use of cyberspace to gain superiority over foes, striking against strategic targets and inflicting violence as a means to achieve policy goals. As competition increases, their advantage over the United States in this area could produce a window of opportunity and increase the likelihood of a strategic level defeat. Those who win the contest for cyber superiority and cyber supremacy will gain a significant advantage in the quest to win future wars. Cyber superiority poses a marked advantage to those who possess it. In the end, the future of the cyber community may well prove to be the difference between victory and defeat in a war not yet fought.

This monograph explores cyber power as a strategic asset. The American cyber community,[5] and the policy makers who guide it, are in a dysfunctional state that is nearing crisis. The United States is far more vulnerable to a strategic defeat in the cyber domain than in any other. Indeed some experts emphasize how the American conventional dominance in other

---

[5] The U.S. cyber community consists of public and private sector professionals with an interest in American posture in cyber space to include visionary hackers, academics and professionals from small and large businesses. This definition was adopted from the Defense Advanced Research Projects Agency, http://www.darpa.mil/NewsEvents/Releases/2011/2011/09/12_DARPA_ENLISTS_CYBER_COMMUNIT C_FOR_FRANK_DISCUSSION.aspx (accessed April 11, 2012).

domains forces opponents to seek asymmetric advantages elsewhere.[6] Cyber warriors can

directly attack civilian infrastructure, industry, and economic targets, breaking the enemy's will.[7]

Their technological focus requires relatively small numbers of personnel and equipment, but

expensive, cutting edge technology that can provide a decisive strategic advantage. However, the

U.S. cyber community's doctrine is sparse, and uniquely within the Department of Defense, it has

been directed to focus on purely defensive measures. In short, American doctrine is failing and

the military's ability to execute it is questionable. The cyber community shares no common

criteria for the selection and education of personnel, and has a sparse funding stream. Equipping

is only now considered a priority within the Department of Defense, and the national military

strategy proscribes the purpose of cyber warfare as merely to maintain the status quo, so

traditional capabilities can be employed unimpeded. In conclusion, the American cyber

community is in search of a common organizational identity, clear mission, and significant means

to positively contribute to our national military strategy and impose our will on future enemies.

This paper will seek to chart a better potential future for the cyber community. Its

ultimate goal is to help chart a road ahead that can close a window of vulnerability and create an

organization that is competitive with its near peer competitors and fills a needed requirement in

the national security community. It acknowledges that in a time of rapid technological advances,

a failure to compete due to organizational inefficiencies and mismanagement will create a gap at

an exponential, vice linear rate. It will examine the community to determine what are the key

attributes that set the cyber community apart and make it distinct from other communities within

the Department of Defense. It will then seek to search for other organizations, currently and in

the recent past, to identify those that shared many of these attributes, yet could still be identified

---

[6] B. H. Liddell Hart, *Strategy, 2nd ed.* (New York: Meridian, 1991), 17

[7] A cyber warrior is a military specialist, law enforcement official, computer forensics expert, or other civil employee who operates within cyber space on the behalf of national interests.

as growing organizations. As will be demonstrated, this paper will determine that two have particularly relevant attributes and are worth further analysis and comparison: the US Army Air Corps of the World War I-World War II interwar period, and the modern day cyber community of Communist China. This paper will look for positive trends that have marked and enabled the success of these two communities. It will then compare and contrast those trends with the modern US cyber community, make a current assessment, and propose recommendations for future growth and organizational change. The goal of this paper is to provide valid analysis that would prove useful to current and future planners and leaders in US CYBERCOM and contribute toward that organization's future role. Ultimately, that role may be the difference between future victory and defeat.

## Strategic Air Power – Historical Case

One of the greatest examples of changes in military technology resulting in organizational change lies in the history of the US Air Force. The development of aviation, and the strategic capabilities that resulted, required new ways of thinking and organizing for war. In fact, development progressed at a rapid pace and the passionate young aviators who wrote of their experiences often stated the potential of air power for the future that it became difficult to distinguish the current reality from the envisioned one.[8] During the interwar period, theorists and leaders found it difficult to make proper decisions in the face of an uncertain future.[9]

Prior to the start of World War I in 1914, the air, unlike the land or sea, was thought to be a benign medium. It was not considered a battleground or environment where a decisive advantage could be gained or lost, to the extent that military commanders thought about it at

---

[8] David MacIsaac, "Voices from the Central Blue: The Air Power Theorists," in *Makers of Modern Strategy from Machiavelli to the Nuclear Age*, ed. Peter Paret, (Princeton, NJ: Princeton University Press, 1986), 626.

[9] Williamson Murray and Allan R. Millett, *Military Innovation in the Interwar Period* (Cambridge, UK: Cambridge University Press, 1996), 124.

all.[10] That a series of visionary leaders would see decisive military advantage to be gained from the skies, and in turn develop organizations, strategies, and weaponry to take such advantage, was a military event rarely seen before or since. The environment under the surface of the ocean and the rise of the U-boat and submarine, and regions of space are other rare examples.

The unprecedented growth of the world's air forces as autonomous military organizations in such an abbreviated period of time serves as an example to other communities. It is the cyber community that has, like aviators of old, come to share a common vision of a battlefield that is around and above us simultaneously. Recently weaponized, such a battlefield has no history, a dynamic present, and an unseen future. How to take advantage of this battlefield is a vitally important question, and we may best look to air forces of the past as a model for organizational change and growth.[11]

Before World War I, generals did not readily appreciate the uses of aviation. Initially, the Signal Corps was the Unites States Army's proponent for heavier than air flight. Aircraft were not weaponized and their chief use was chiefly unarmed reconnaissance. Since an airplane was not seen as a "weapon," generals who saw war as a contest of wills between armed combatants devoted little thought to the potential of the aircraft. During the period 1903 to 1914, aircraft had limited capability in terms of ceiling and range, and virtually no payload. They were initially employed much as balloons were employed in the 19th century. Significantly, manned aircraft performed a significant role in the 1914 Battle of The Marne, providing the French Army with early warning of German advances.[12]

World War I brought great changes, and new concepts. The first was weaponization. More powerful engines enabled airplanes to carry cameras and drop bombs. Aircraft were soon

---

[10] Michael S. Sherry, *The Rise of American Air Power: The Creation of Armageddon* (New Haven, CT: Yale University Press, 1989), 5.

[11] MacIsaac, "Voices from the Central Blue: The Air Power Theorists," 634.

[12] Barbara W. Tuchman, *The Guns of August* (New York: Ballantine Books, 1962), 412.

equipped with machine guns and could now engage in aerial combat with each other. The ability of the airplane to kill, especially targeting ground forces, caused contemporary generals to recognize its status as a weapon, and interest in bombers and their employment increased exponentially.[13] Increased use led to the beginnings of tactics, techniques and procedures for their employment: reconnaissance aircraft required escort, bombers could target the enemy rear battle area, and fighters could destroy other fighters and allow or prevent operations of other friendly aircraft. Air superiority became a goal for condition setting in order to allow reconnaissance, attacks against enemy troops, and protection of friendly forces from enemy strikes. Air superiority became a prerequisite for ground forces to maximize their chances for decisive victory. Air campaigns by airmen were fought to achieve this superiority, and so influenced the ground fight. With a weaponized airplane, leaders and theorists focused on a piece of equipment that was now a lethal weapon system. And with that focus, came debate and discord.[14]

The achievements of World War I caused theorists to conceptualize new and greater possible uses. The politically unacceptable loss of life and financial costs of ground combat overseas caused leaders, both political and military, to search for cheaper, more creative alternatives.[15] The military chiefs of the leading powers all pursued air forces. While most air power theorist advocated the use of strategic bombing to strike at the enemy industrial base, it was Billy Mitchell's ideal of an autonomous air force command that centralized coordination of all air assets that freed it from the control of the army.[16]

---

[13] Irving B. Holley Jr., *Ideas and Weapons*, (Ann Arbor, MI: University of Michigan, 1983), 85.

[14] David E. Johnson, *Fast Tanks and Heavy Bombers: Innovation in the U.S. Army, 1917-1945,* (Ithaca: Cornell University Press, 1998), 82.

[15] MacIssac, "Voices from the Central Blue: The Air Power Theorists," 626.

[16] Ibid., 631.

During the interwar period, the air communities in both the United States and United

Kingdom believed that "the bomber would always get through" and that civilian infrastructure

could be rendered defenseless, and could, in turn, justify greater expenditures on aircraft, as

opposed to land armies.[17] Based on this basic assumption, there was an agreed upon belief that

building an offensive capability could provide deterrence against rival air forces. If the offense

was inherently superior to defense, spending scarce resources on defensive measures was fruitless

and wasteful.[18] If airpower, directed against factories and resources, offered a decisive path to

victory, a refusal to resource such a technology could amount to national suicide. In the face of

uncertainty, aviation leaders in their respective nations advocated for greater resources and

autonomy as a deterrent against future adversaries, and an uncertain future. The desire for

aviation leaders to make such an assessment, that one form of aerial warfare was stronger than

another, and allocate resources accordingly, was a factor that encouraged a drive toward an air

force independent of other services, capable of developing its own doctrine free from external

interference.[19]

In practice 'outsiders' can seldom exert a direct influence on military reform because they

lack full knowledge of the difficulties and options available. On the other hand, the responsible

military authorities tend to be all too well aware of the problems and to accept that only

piecemeal or compromise measures are feasible…most important of all, the interwar period bears

out the Clauswitzian perception that political attitudes, priorities, and constraints exert a

dominating influence on the development of armed forces and strategic doctrines.[20]

---

[17] Richard Overy, *Why the Allies Won,* (New York: W. W. Norton & Company, 1995), 104.

[18] Warren A. Trest, *Air Force Roles and Missions: A History* (Washington, DC: Air Force History and Museums Program, 1998), 49.

[19] Herman S. Wolk, *Toward Independence: The Emergence of the U.S. Air Force, 1945-1947,* (Washington, DC: Air Force History and Museums Program, 1996), 2.

[20] Johnson, *Fast Tanks and Heavy Bombers,* 14.

In the United States, the Army and Navy had different perspectives on air power's future missions, doctrine and organization which caused U.S. Army Air Corps leaders to press for greater independence.[21] Brigadier General Billy Mitchell's experiments against captured German ships, proving modern capital ships could be destroyed from the air, provided evidence that aviation had great potential.[22] The not-so-subtle argument grew that those whose careers began and thrived in aviation understood its capabilities better than outsiders. These leaders, to increase their future budgets, promoted civil applications, such as the flying of air mail following a two year Congressional investigation into the corruption of federal air mail contracts. President Franklin Roosevelt's 1934 executive order designating the Army Air Corps to fly air mail was a public relations achievement and, despite early crashes, increased the cohesion of the fledgling air force and its confidence in its leaders.[23]

Opposition by leaders such as General Douglas MacArthur, the Chief of Staff of the Army, prompted further debate. MacArthur wanted to see more of the scarce budget devoted to ground forces, but aviators justified their position by arguing that MacArthur, a non-aviator, did not have the expertise to decide on such a future course for new technology.[24] The question arose as to whether in an era of technological change, those within this community could better argue for capabilities against those who had no training or experience. Such arguments caused cohesion within the Army Air Corps to grow. A by-product of this debate was that professional judgments became personal, an officer's expertise as a pilot was construed by some as a

---

[21] Trest, *Air Force Roles and Missions: A History*, 67.

[22] Alfred F. Hurley, *Billy Mitchell: Crusader for Air Power* (Bloomington: Indiana University Press, 1975), 68.

[23] W. David Lewis, "Edward V. Rickenbacker's Reaction to Civil Aviation Policy in the 1930s: A Hidden Dimension," in *Reconsidering a Century of Flight,* ed. Roger D. Launius and Janet R. Daly Bedarek, (Chapel Hill, NC: University of North Carolina Press, 2003), 124

[24] James P. Tate, *The Army and Its Air Corps: Army Policy toward Aviation, 1919-1941* (Washington, DC: U.S. Government Printing Office, 1998), 135.

prerequisite for a sound argument.[25]  Aviators argued that those who did not have personal experience in the air were not qualified to make budgeting decisions.  Technological development was cost intensive, technologically intensive, and took place far faster than in the ground branches of the Army.  Aircraft that were developed twenty years apart bore little resemblance to each other, while artillery, rifles, and machine guns were almost exactly the same.  The vast difference in procurement for ground and sea forces, vice procurement for aviation, created a fissure that detracted from a common frame of reference and contributed toward independent-mindedness among airpower advocates.[26]

New theorists took advantage of the horrors of World War I to describe how aviation could solve the problems of the trench for future war.  In 1921, Italian General Guilio Douhet provided the early articulation of strategic warfare theory.  In his book, *Command of the Air,* Douhet argued that the vastness of the sky made defense against air attack impossible.  Because of this, airpower was inherently offensive and could dominate land and sea operations.  "To conquer the command of the air means victory; to be beaten in the air means defeat and acceptance of whatever terms the enemy may be pleased to impose."[27]  Air supremacy would be used to strike at the will of the people by destroying the nation's "vital centers."  Douhet identified these vital centers as industry, transportation, communications, government centers, and the will of the people.  He stressed that the morale of the civilian population was important to affecting the enemy's will to wage war.[28]  In Douhet's theory, national defense could only be assured by an independent Air Force of adequate power.  Moreover, air forces were not relegated to setting the conditions for the success of ground forces, as was seen in World War I.  They

---

[25] Johnson, *Fast Tanks and Heavy Bombers*, 82.

[26] Trest, *Air Force Roles and Missions: A History*, 66.

[27] Giulio Douhet and Dino Ferrari, *The Command of the Air* (Washington, DC: Air Force History and Museums Program, 1998; 1942), 28

[28] Ibid., 47-48

could bring war to an enemy civilian population, break an enemy's will, bring a nation to its knees, and thereby achieve political goals independent of other lines of operation.

Largely based on Douhet's theory and their experiences observing troop movements, supporting ground action, and even strategic bombing in the last two years of World War I, the British and American air power champions looked to pursue the realization of this untested theory.[29] Although must speculation on air power theory was discussed during the interwar period, it was not tested until World War II. This was acknowledged by the American author of the strategic bombing campaign in Europe, Major General Haywood S. Hansell, Jr.: "The road ahead promised to be a stormy one. Feasibility of effective and sustained air attack as the key to victory could not be demonstrated by past experience. Victory through air power alone was pure theory."[30] Billy Mitchell and other such champions of airpower viewed planners who argued for alternative strategies of allocating resources as obstacles and opposition.[31]

The interwar period showed the growth of the doctrine and organizational structure that reflected this theory and, as technological advances were realized, the specialization of aircraft to meet tactical, operational, and strategic needs. The capabilities and limitations of a strategic bomber were radically different from a fighter plane, and the decisions as to how many to procure of each, the priorities as to training, employment, and budgeting were the sorts of decisions that leaders and planners could not make without a lifetime of relevant expertise and experience. The Army's air arm grew from a division within the Signal Corps, to a separate combat branch of the Army, to one of the three major army commands.[32] As the US Army Air Corps expanded, a

---

[29] Wolk, *Toward Independence: The Emergence of the U.S. Air Force, 1945-1947*, 1.

[30] Haywood S. Hansell, *The Air Plan that Defeated Hitler* (Atlanta: Higgins-McArthur/Longino & Porter, 1979), 75.

[31] Hurley, *Billy Mitchell: Crusader for Air Power*, 100.

[32] The Army's Air Arm was established as the Aeronautical Division of the Signal Corps in 1907; reorganized as the Aviation Section of the Signal Corps in 1914; redesignated a combat branch of the Army, the Army Air Service, by the Reorganization Act of 1920; named the Army Air Corps in 1926;

variety of organizational factors, many of which have a common frame of reference with today's cyber environment, caused the organization to change in predictable, logical ways. An examination of these factors and causes is useful to future leaders and theorists as they look at the future of cyber warfare.

The first factor was the perceived demand. The art of war circa 1918 was a flawed instrument. Coercing a potential enemy without resorting to trench warfare was popular among politicians and leaders. Ground combat was expensive, and casualties exacted an unacceptable political cost. A community that offered an alternative would find its voice heard. The demand for an alternative helped provide resources to the USAAC, and provide a platform for its leaders and theorists. Expertise in airpower provided these leaders with a seat at the table where their arguments drew support.[33]

A second major factor was the pace of technological growth in aviation, which outstripped the pace in other services. Unlike ground forces, where many weapons changed little from World War I to World War II, technological advances grew at a rapid pace. New aircraft were constantly in development to take advantage of innovation in construction, engines, and armaments. Aviation captured a spirit of adventure through the achievements of both military and civilian personnel, most notably Charles Lindbergh's flight from New York to Paris.[34] Records for speed, range, and altitude were broken at a rapid pace.[35]

---

renamed the Army Air Forces by Army Regulation 95-5 in 1941; before being reorganized as one of the three major army commands by the War Department in 1942. Summarized from Thomas H. Greer, *The Development of Air Doctrine in the Army Air Arm, 1917-1941,* (Washington, DC: Office of Air Force History, U.S. Air Force, 1985).

[33] Maurer Maurer, *Aviation in the U.S. Army, 1919-1939*, (Washington, DC: United States Air Force Historical Research Center, 1987), 200.

[34] Ibid., 255.

[35] David B. Thurston, *The World's Most Significant and Magnificent Aircraft: Evolution of the Modern Airplane*, (Warrendale, PA: Society of Automotive Engineers, 2000), 156.

A third factor was the second and third order effects that technological growth prompted. Theorists could effectively communicate a believable vision of future aviation, and future potential that was ambitious, yet believable to the public when the rapid growth of aviation was considered. Like the growth of the computer in the past thirty years, decision makers could readily appreciate the rapid technological advances they had personally witnessed in their own lifetimes, and could be easily convinced of greater and equally achievable effects in the immediate future. Such advances fostered great cohesion among Mitchell, Hansell, Alexander de Seversky, and the other "true believers" of aviation, who could see in their profession the possibilities of a unique, war-winning capability.[36] A realization that change was occurring at a rapid tempo could justify making strategic decisions based on minimal hard data, as a way of mitigating the risk of making a decision too late at all. The amount of resources that were poured into strategic bombing capabilities, for example, were considerable given the lack of hard data that could predict whether it would be successful, or not.[37]

The fourth factor is that increasing competition for money and resources, coupled with the upstart organization's belief in its own future relevance and strategic organization, caused conflict. Army leadership disagreed on missions, budget, and supporting/supported relationships. The Army emphasized personnel end strength over mechanization and technology. MacArthur outlined his position, "It is easy, of course, to emphasize the influence of machinery in war. It is man that makes war, not machines, and the human element must always remain the dominant

---

[36] Williamson Murray and Allan R. Millett, *Military Innovation in the Interwar Period* (Cambridge, UK: Cambridge University Press, 1996), 188.

[37] Between 1933 and 1937 the spending for army aviation increased from $25.2 to $59.4 million and naval aviation rose from $25.2 million to $38.5 million while the overall budgets for both services decreased. How to employ air forces was widely debated between the service leaders and air power advocates. For details of these debates see Trest, *Air Force Roles and Missions: A History,* 65-81.

one."[38] After the Army Air Corps fought to gain organizational structure and manning, it had to continue to fight to establish its role in war.

The issue over human factors is a difficult one to address fully within the scope of this paper; traditional generals such as MacArthur believed that the human element would remain dominant.[39] However, much popular sentiment opposed this viewpoint. The human element seemed to matter little when the horrors of the machine gun, artillery piece, and other elements of trench warfare demanded such loss of life for little gain. Technological answers to foreign policy questions, such as a strategic bomber to compel an enemy to submit to our will, were seen as better solutions than a mass army of conscripts that would suffer grievously for an indecisive result. The populations of the interwar period wanted peace, and failing that, an increased assurance that the horrors of trench warfare would not be repeated. Trench warfare had shown that weapons and technology had severely limited the role of human will and choice; aircraft were an impersonal, technological solution to an impersonal, technological problem. A cheap solution to how to circumvent the trench appealed to popular imagination; by threatening the role of infantry generals such as MacArthur it prompted yet greater fissures between aviation communities and the land power advocates.[40]

A sixth factor is a conservative course of action that maintained aviation in a supporting role chafed the leadership of the Army Air Corps. It created a super-charged organization made up of individuals who believed they were on the cutting edge of the future of warfare. Inspired by Billy Mitchell and other early leaders, they sought ways to prove the value of airpower so that

---

[38] Johnson, *Fast Tanks and Heavy Bombers*, 113.

[39] Ibid., 113.

[40] Avoiding trench warfare by employing a capability that could provide "quick, clean, mechanical and impersonal solutions" such as strategic bombing was the politically preferred method as addressed by MacIsaac in "Voices from the Central Blue: The Air Power Theorists," 626. General MacArthur believed that air power should be employed in support of ground actions as addressed in Maurer, *Aviation in the U.S. Army, 1919-1939*, 288.

14

it could reach a potential that many did not fully comprehend yet.  These leaders effectively achieved support from their subordinates on the need for independent air force, which had access to its own ownership of doctrine, revenue, procurement, and education.[41]

A seventh factor is that the role of education cannot be underestimated.  Setting up a school where airpower doctrine could be taught independent of centralized Army oversight was an important step to reinforcing a shared vision, and doctrine.  This is an important point in the corporate identity of any growing organization.  The leaders of the Army Air Corps believed that in the face of opposition from outside viewpoints, it was important to place its best thinkers in the training establishment so that as the organization expanded, future leaders could share a common appreciation for potential uses.  Lieutenant Colonel John F. Curry, the commander of the Army Air Forces Tactical School, wanted the school at Maxwell Field to be a "clearing house where tactical ideas can flow, where they can be tried and where the doctrine can go out to the service to be put into practice and evaluated."[42]  It was the instructors at this school who created the theory that would dominate the air power debate.[43]  He argued that modern nations were highly dependent on industrial production to wage war and that this situation created an "industrial web" of interdependent components.  Modern industrial nations were susceptible to defeat by the interruption of this web.  He believed that this interruption via strategic bombing was the primary objective of an air force.[44]  American doctrine during this time highlights this argument and couples it with Douhet's belief that striking forces could penetrate enemy defenses and drop

---

[41] Murray and Millett, *Military Innovation in the Interwar Period*, 359.

[42] Ibid., 155.

[43] Wesley F. Craven and James L. Cate, *The Army Air Forces in World War II,* (Chicago: USAF Historical Division, 1948), 51-52.  Major Donald Wilson and Major Muir Fairchild were responsible for the extensive development of the industrial web theory as a part of the ACTS Bombardment Course at the Army Air Forces Tactical School in the mid-to-late-1930s.

[44] Johnson, *Fast Tanks and Heavy Bombers*, 161.

bombs without unacceptable losses.[45] In the late 1930s, the use of strategic bombing dominated the American air power argument.

Cyber warfare professionals are generally averse to the study of history and the humanities in general, but the computer oriented principle of "garbage in, garbage out" is widely acclaimed.[46] The ability to establish a school that uses facts, data points, historical events, and generate valid theories and doctrine may well be the essential peacetime task, just like the establishment of a codified doctrine center of excellence at Maxwell Field in the 1930s was a vital step in the development of the US Air Force.[47] By forcing aspiring aviators to enter the Air Corps as second lieutenants, and placing those deemed by the organization as its "best and brightest" in the education and doctrine field where ideas were promoted, the Army Air Corps rapidly developed into a cohesive community that possessed a shared vision for the future and belief in itself and its capabilities.

Another important factor was the American aviators saw other air forces achieve successes in their respective countries. The Royal Air Force was a successful independent air force, and American leaders coveted a similar level of autonomy. The United States readily acknowledged that other organizations, specifically the German Luftwaffe, were better developed and organized in all respects. Although the Luftwaffe was not officially established until 1935 when Adolf Hitler violated the Treaty of Versailles, the German government invested money and

---

[45] Trest, *Air Force Roles and Missions: A History*, 65.

[46] The "garbage in, garbage out" principle is commonly used in the computer science and information technology fields. It is based on the observation that good inputs results in good outcomes and bad inputs result in bad outputs. This is as defined by William Lidwell, Kritina Holden and Jill Butler in *Universal Principles of Design 11ᵗʰ ed.*, (Beverly, MA: Rockport Publishers, 2010), 112. Many in the military computer science, information technology and related fields subscribe to the thoughts Dr. Edward Brush of the University of Maryland who states ". . .history and science are inherently different kinds of disciplines; bringing them together is likely to do violence to one or the other..." from Paul E. Ceruzzi, "The Challenge of Introducing History into a Computer Science Curriculum," 27-32, *Using History To Teach Computer Science and Related Disciplines*, (Washington, DC: Computing Research Association, 2004), 30.

[47] Johnson, *Fast Tanks and Heavy Bombers*, 155.

manpower in the development of the air power in the USSR. The Germans established a squadron at the Lipetsk Airfield in 1924 that was almost entirely made up of Luftwaffe military aircraft and crews.[48] These early investments allowed the Luftwaffe to quickly dominate the skies over Europe. This perceived threat helped justify increased money for the growing American air force.

American aviation theorists emphasized the lack of a credible strategic bomber. The development of the B-17 Flying Fortress was seen as an unstoppable weapon that could fight its way through the defenses of any foreign country. It was a four engine bomber that combined great range, defensive firepower, and could carry a heavy bomb load. Aviators believed it could fly deep into enemy countries, protect itself from their air forces, and drop enough bombs to destroy important targets. It could, in short, make the theories a reality. [49] The presence of a perceived capability that justified and validated theorists such as Douhet, and politicians who claimed "the bomber will always get through," prompted more aggressive expansion goals.[50] Significantly, the early theorists at Maxwell Field who pioneered the theory of strategic bombing were the ones rapidly promoted into positions to make decisions about future technological developments.

There were downsides to this development. The offensive capability of strategic bombardment was the core competency, or unique capability that the Air Corps brought to the US Military that justified a more independent role and mission set. However, there was a disconnect between theory and practice. Then-Major Claire Chennault, for one, was a critic of the theory

---

[48] Robin D. Higham and Stephen J. Harris, *Why Air Forces Fail: The Anatomy of Defeat* (Lexington, KY: University of Kentucky Press, 2006), 205.

[49] Eric M. Bergerud, *Fire in the Sky: The Air War in the South Pacific* (Boulder, CO: Westview Press, 2000), 232.

[50] This is from Stanley Baldwin's speech on disarmament to the House of Commons on November 10, 1932. "I think it is well also for the man in the street to realize that there is no power on earth that can protect him from being bombed, whatever people may tell him. The bomber will always get through." Full text can be found at http://airminded.org/2007/11/10/the-bomber-will-always-get-through/.

that the bomber would always get through. He believed air defenses could defeat bomber attacks, and therefore bombers would require fighter escorts However, fighter escorts with equivalent range to accompany the bombers and defeat the defenders were impractical at the time due to insufficient fuel and other technological limitations. Many fighters were also too slow. [51] The point being that the organization stifled Chennault's divergent but correct thoughts, not the incorrect ones of the air force and their vision statement.

The development of the B-17 bears important lessons for today. The theory and ideas behind its use preceded the contemporary technical and tactical capability. Development of doctrine, schools, and a common understanding of how to plan and lead such an effort preceded the construction of the aircraft. Airmen who had years of experience and great expertise were able to make sound generally sound decisions as to the development of the aircraft and had an appreciation of how to use it. Had the B-17 and other heavy bombers in general been technologically feasible in the 1920s, it is questionable whether its capability would have been used to the fullest. Organizations that did not have a sound base of education, training, and thought could have looked at this capability and marginalized it. The Luftwaffe, for example, had preconceived notions that the airpower should chiefly support ground forces. Although they had a similar industrial capacity they chose to focus on less-capable tactical bombers that had two engines, not four, and carried a smaller payload.[52]

The conclusions we can draw from these factors indicate that in a rapidly expanding technical field or service, that doctrine, education, and strategic planning must be in place first, to guide the development, procurement, and use of technology. Another lesson learned is in the Air Force's understanding of deterrence—the ability to prevent an enemy from seeking to strike a blow, due to their fear of a strong counterattack. Deterrence must be credible to prevent an

---

[51] Johnson, *Fast Tanks and Heavy Bombers*, 157.

[52] Higham and Harris, *Why Air Forces Fail: The Anatomy of Defeat*, 212.

opponent from making an attack. Generally speaking, a deterrent that is similar in execution to the threat posed will be more credible. [53] It is easy to see, for example how the threat of a strategic bombing capability could deter a rival. It is harder to visualize how a strong army or navy would deter an air force. Once strategic bombardment was perceived as a credible threat, a American capability was required to deter others. The limits of technology in World War II had an effect on airpower development. The Germans did not have a strategic capability to defeat the Royal Air Force in the Battle of Britain, or the capability to attack American soil at all. Their bombers did not have the defensive firepower, range, or payload of the B-17, and could not successfully destroy targets over England in the face of RAF defenses. Strategic bombardment was a "one way street" which sapped German resources. [54] In the Pacific theater, the American ability to bombard the Japanese mainland, to include the final strikes with atomic weapons, was a capability without counter that precluded a bloody ground invasion. [55] Likewise, cyber warfare can be a "one way street" if future competitors create an offensive capability we can neither defend against or deter.

Later this paper will examine the specific circumstances of Air Force expansion in the interwar years, and determine what aspects of the development are most applicable to the cyber community circa 2012. Several facts are readily apparent: Military leaders have historically focused on technologies after, not before, they are weaponized. Air Forces had limited historical background data, yet a rapid rate of technological growth. Political sentiment left leaders open to new, untested ideas. Having an educational, personnel, and doctrinal baseline contributed to the cohesiveness of the air power community and its supporters and showed that the community was

---

[53] Lawrence Freedman, *Deterrence* (Cambridge, UK: Polity Press, 2004), 30-32.

[54] John Keegan, *Intelligence in War: The Value and Limitations of What the Military Can Learn About the Enemy* (New York: Vintage Books, 2002), 268.

[55] Robert A. Pape, *Bombing to Win: Air Power and Coercion in War* (Ithaca, NY: Cornell University Press, 1996), 87.

in line with their leader's vision. Lastly, the presence of near-peer competitors that had taken advantage of this technology fostered a desire, based on fear and the perception that offense was more powerful than defense, to keep pace or face calamity. Such pressure is easily evident today.

## The Rise of Cyber Power

Cyber warfare has been defined by government security expert Richard A. Clarke, in his book *Cyber War*, as "actions by a nation-state to penetrate another nation's computers or networks for the purposes of causing damage or disruption."[56] The computers and networks are essential to process, store and transmit the information of individuals and groups. It is this information, expanding to commercial industry, essential services, governments, and organizations that runs the world as we know it today. The criticality of the network to the US Army became apparent with the adoption of the Network Centric Warfare concept.[57] By moving the synchronization of the battlefield to the network, it opened itself to a host of unintended consequences. In 2010, The New York Times reported that "a secret cyber war arms race is under way as a number of countries build sophisticated software and hardware attack capabilities."[58]

Coordinated cyber attacks can shape the larger battlespace and influence a wide range of forces and levers of power in the next war.[59] Early forms of this have already been seen in attacks in Estonia and Georgia. Both of these attacks were suspected to be initiated by Russia.. Cyber supremacy may thus be as decisive in the network-dependent twenty-first century as air

---

[56] Richard A. Clarke and Robert K. Knake, *Cyber War* (New York: Harper Collins, 2010), 6.

[57] Network centric warfare is a concept that "…focuses on the combat power that can be generated from the effective linking or networking of the warfighting enterprise. It is characterized by the ability of geographically dispersed forces (consisting of entities) to create a high level of shared battlespace awareness that can be exploited via self-synchronization and other network-centric operations to achieve commanders' intent." This definition is from David Alberts, John J. Garstka, and Frederick P. Stein, *Network Centric Warfare: Developing and Leveraging Information Superiority 2nd Ed.* (Washington, DC: DoD C4ISR Cooperative Research Program, 1999), 89.

[58] John Markoff, "A Code for Chaos." *The New York Times*, October 3, 2010, http://www.nytimes.com/2010/10/03/weekinreview/03markoff.html (accessed February 1, 2012).

[59] A cyber attack is deliberate exploitation of computer systems, technology-dependent enterprises and networks.

supremacy was for most of the twentieth century. According to the February 2010, Quadrennial Defense Review, although it is a man-made domain, "cyberspace is now as relevant for DoD activities as the naturally occurring domains of land, sea, air, and space."[60] The American concern is a valid, but late assessment of the quickly escalating nature of cyber war.

There are more contemporary examples to examine the escalation of warfare in the cyber realm. In the recent past there have been multiple successful examples of cyber attacks at the operational and strategic level; the demand is increasing, and based on a track record of success. A second factor that is applying to cyber warfare that is shared with strategic bombing is that the pace of technological development is very rapid, and a time lag in developing this capability poses great risks. A third factor that was shared with airpower theorists is that in an age of rapid growth, with perceived demand, there will be conflict between budgeting growth in cyber vs. more traditional threats. The data from these recent examples reinforce the validity of the factors that would contribute toward a more independent cyber community.

In the 2006 war against Hezbollah, Israel alleged that cyber-warfare was significant part of the conflict. The Israel Defense Force intelligence estimated that several countries in the Middle East used Russian hackers and scientists to operate on Hezbollah's behalf. As a result, Israel has attached growing importance to cyber-tactics, and became, along with the United States, France, China, and a number of other nations, involved in cyber-war planning. In the Israeli case a disappointing operation in Lebanon prompted openness to new ideas. As will be seen, their willingness to attack enemy computer networks helped them significantly in 2007.

In September 2007, Israel carried out an airstrike on Syria dubbed Operation Orchard. American industry and military sources speculated that the Israelis may have used cyber warfare to allow their planes to pass undetected by radar into Syria. This addition of a cyber capability to

---

[60] US Department of Defense, "Quadrennial Defense Review February 2010," under "QDR 2010," www.defense.gov/qdr/images/QDR_as_of_12Feb10_1000.pdf (accessed October 13, 2011), 37.

a combined arms attack is similar to the suppression or destruction of air defenses to allow follow-on attacks by artillery and electronic jamming. The advantage of using a cyber attack to disable the radars is that it allowed the Israelis to truly surprise the Syrians.[61] Prior to Operation Orchard an air strike would have been preceded by active jamming, suppression of enemy air defense strikes, or a lethal strike through other means, such as AH-64 helicopters in operation Desert Storm. The Israeli attack, using computers and code to disrupt the operation of Syrian radar computers, enabled a surprise kinetic strike. Using cyber capability to make a conventional attack easier is easily visualized by Pentagon leadership. However, while such cyber attacks were a supporting effort in a larger operation that created lethal effects, the Israeli attacks were generally traditional attempts to "hack" the Syrian air defense systems, not lethal strikes of their own.[62] Their ability to suppress enemy air defense systems was more efficient then a sizeable armada of World War II bombers.

The tensions between Israel and its adversaries appear to be escalating. While Iran invested a reported one billion dollars to hire computer experts to build their offensive and defensive cyber capabilities, the IDF continues to build on the past successes and has increased their own cyber capability. Lately, Israel has recruited three hundred young computer prodigies to serve as cyber warfare soldiers.[63] They have learned from Hezbollah's attacks in 2006. The Estonian's learned in 2007 the significance of an attack on their infrastructure. Unfortunately for them, they had to defend themselves from a strike far stronger than anything Israel faced.

---

[61] David A. Fulghum and Douglas Barrie. "Israel used electronic attack in air strike against Syrian mystery target," *Aviation Week & Space Technology*, October 8, 2007, under "Operation Orchard" http://www.aviationweek.com/aw/generic/story.jsp?channel=defense&id=news/aw100807p2.xml&headline=Israel%20used%20electronic%20attack%20in%20air%20strike%20against%20Syrian%20mystery%20target&prev=10 (accessed on January 10, 2012).

[62] Jeffrey Carr, *Cyber Warfare: Mapping the Cyber Underworld* (Sebastopol, CA: O'Reilly Media, 2011), 251.

[63] Tiffany Gabbay, "Israeli Defense Forces Build Elite Hacker Team Amid Growing Cyber-Warfare Threat," January 13, 2012, under "Israeli Cyber," http://www.theblaze.com/stories/israeli-defense-forces-build-elite-hacker-team-amid-growing-cyber-warfare-threat/ (accessed January 13, 2012).

Cyber war escalated to state-on-state punitive action in 2007 in Estonia. In February of

that year, the Estonian legislature passed a law that required anything honoring the time they were

occupied by the Soviet Union to be taken down. Tensions between ethnic Russians living in

Estonia and native Estonians had been building since Estonia declared its independence at the end

of the Cold War. Although the Estonian president vetoed the law, tensions spilled out into the

streets on April 27. "Bronze Night" as it became known, saw clashes between factions around

the base of the Bronze Soldier of Tallinn statue, a Soviet World War II monument honoring the

Soviet victory over Nazi Germany but seen by Estonians as another symbol of Soviet

occupation.[64] When the authorities intervened, they moved the statue to a new location within a

military cemetery. Instead of suppressing the tensions, it ignited nationalist responses in the

Russian media and legislature. Shortly after Bronze Night, Estonia's main computer servers that

ran the public infrastructure, banking, commerce, government sites, and internet access came

under cyber attack.[65] This distributed denial of service attack flooded the Estonian servers with

cyber access requests, causing them to collapse under the load and shut down. The largest

numbers of attacks were coming from Russia and from official servers of the Russian

government.[66] While normally such an attack is considered a nuisance, the one in Estonia was the

largest ever seen.[67] These attacks did not just hit public websites, but over a million computers

attacked the IP addresses, the logical addresses used to uniquely identify every computer in the

network that most people would not readily identify; the telephone network, credit card

verification systems, government ministries, the internet directory, banks, and the media were all

---

[64] BBC News, "Tallinn Tense After Deadly Riots," April 28, 2007. *BBC News*, London, UK. http://news.bbc.co.uk/2/hi/europe/6602171.stm (accessed April 3, 2012).

[65] Matt Murphy, "War in the Fifth Domain. Are the Mouse and Keyboard the New Weapons of Conflict?," *The Economist*. July 1, 2010, under "Cyberwar: War in the Fifth Domain," http://www.economist.com/node/16478792 (accessed on 21 January 2012).

[66] Arthur Bright, "Estonia Accuses Russia of 'Cyber Attack,'" *The Christian Science Monitor*. May 17, 2007. http://www.csmonitor.com/2007/0517/p99s01-duts.html (accessed 14 January 2012).

[67] Clarke and Knake, *Cyber War*, 14.

targeted.[68]  These attacks resulted in a major disruption to the Estonian way of life.  Those who could get to work, had difficulty doing their jobs.  Citizens could not shop, bank, call their family, or surf the internet.

The attacks went on for weeks.  Even as experts applied countermeasures that were successful on smaller attacks, the attacks kept coming.  In Estonia, hundreds of key sites were being hit week after week and were unable to restore normal service. Cyber experts traced the attacks back to controlling machines that had millions of "zombie" computers under their command.  The computer code involved was written on Russian-alphabet keyboards, which Estonia government officials said was proof of Russian involvement.  While the Russian government initially denied any involvement, they later stated that it was possible some "patriotic Russians" took matters into their own hands.[69]

The Estonia cyber attack proved that cyber could be a major factor in disrupting a government's operations as well as the daily activities of an entire population.  This is significant for the future of cyber war because it does not clearly point to a particular responsible attacker. The future of warfare will involve actors that may or may not be sponsored by nation-states.  The motivations will be mystifying.  In the Estonian case, it could have been outraged hackers acting on their own, overzealous Russian patriots, the Russian mafia, hired hackers operating on behalf of the government or someone else, or it could have been a combination of any of the above or none of the above.  Given the uncertain identity of the attacker, any retaliation could potentially target the wrong source.  The secretive nature of cyber war adds an additional level of complexity to the environment, as it is hard to retaliate when attribution is unclear.

---

[68] Clark Boyd, "Cyber-war a Growing Threat Warn Experts." *BBC News.* June 17, 2010. http://www.bbc.co.uk/news/10339543 (accessed on 16 January 2012).

[69] Clarke and Knake, *Cyber War*, 16.

Significantly, the attack on Estonian targets, unlike the Israeli effort, can be seen as "policy by other means," a less then lethal effort to coerce a rival state to submit to the will of another, to effect Russian policy. While the technical assessment of damage to Estonian systems may seem minor, and therefore of little interest to a military audience, this attack shows the ability of cyber warfare to fit into a Clauswitzian model of a pursuit of policy through other means. Douhet would have appreciated the Russians' ability to break the Estonian will, like a bomber offensive, a cyber attack destroyed Estonian infrastructure. Pandora's Box continued to open as the utility of an offensive cyber capability cheaply and quickly coerced Estonian policymakers.

Cyber war saw another demonstration when Georgian sites were attacked by hackers during the 2008 South Ossetia War. Following a month of military buildup, airfield improvements and railroad repairs, the Russians conducted military exercises that moved forces into position along the Georgian border. July brought overt airspace violation and numerous cyber attacks. The uniqueness of this campaign was that Russia used sustained, synchronized kinetic and cyber-attacks against the Georgian government and people. [70]

Like any military action, preparation for the cyber attack included reconnaissance, mapping, and planning. The Russian cyber experts, in this case government and criminal factions, already had ways into key information strong holds. They had attack scripts, clean domain registrations and entirely new, undetected websites prepositioned.[71] These sorts of preparations required significant time, manpower, and resources. It indicates that the Russian

---

[70] Dancho Danchev, "Coordinated Russia vs Georgia Cyberattack," *ZDnet.* August 8, 2008. http://www.zdnet.com/blog/security/coordinated-russia-vs-georgia-cyber-attack-in-progress/1670. (accessed February 1, 2012).

[71] David J. Smith and Khatuna Mshvisobadze, "Russia, Georgia and the Shape of Cyber Wars to Come," (Presentation, SMi Cyber Security Forum Initiative, Istanbul, May 16, 2011).

capability did not spring up overnight. It also indicates that a capability such as this cannot be improvised without planning, recruiting, and the time to establish a capable organization.

On August 7, 2008, a large number of Georgian internet servers were attacked and taken over by external entities. When the ground war broke out on August 8, cyber attacks essentially blinded and silenced the Georgian government. Through distributed denial of service attacks, many of which were similar to the ones used in the Estonian attack, the Georgian government was unable to counter Russian international information operations campaign. Redirection of official government sites to Russian proxy sites, led to confusion in the government, among the people of Georgia and international audiences. This intentional misinformation delayed international response to the Russian invasion. [72]

Once the South Ossentia Province was occupied, the Russian Business Network, a Russian organized crime network that specializes in cybercrime, executed a cyber blockade that routed Georgian internet traffic through Russia and denied Georgia its cyber independence. Targeted internet traffic and websites included the American and British Embassies in Tbilisi, the Georgian Parliament, Ministry of Foreign Affairs, Supreme Court, news agencies, the Central Election Commission and others.[73] Georgian-based access to the BBC and CNN websites were redirected to fake BBC and CNN reports. The Russian Business Network, believed to be in cooperation with the Russian government, mastered the art of synchronizing operations through time, space, and purpose.

The Georgian cyber attacks marked another escalation in cyber warfare in that the attacks were coordinated with military maneuvers on the ground and were openly attributable to a government; the Russians disrupted Georgian access to information, and successfully conducted

---

[72] John Markoff, "Before the Gunfire, Cyberattacks," *The New York Times*, August 12, 2008. http://www.nytimes.com/2008/08/13/technology/13cyber.html (accessed January 31, 2012).

[73] Republic of Georgia, "Russian Invasion of Georgia," www.georgiaupdate.gov.ge (accessed December 24, 2011).

deception operations via interception of "trusted" global media news sites. This use of deception is an increasingly used tactic in cyber war. The deception efforts, coupled with synchronization between cyber attacks and ground offensives (themselves a leap forward from Israeli synchronization efforts) demonstrated the new potential. Furthermore, a significant cyber attack again proved that "The megabyte would always get through," and that defensive measures were inadequate to defeat or prevent a surprise cyber attack. The megabyte got through, and circumvented traditional defenses to undermine the ability of the Georgian military to resist.

In May 2010, in response to the hacker group named the Indian Cyber Army defacing Pakistani websites, over one thousand Indian websites were defaced by a number of hacker groups.[74] Hacked sites included the Brahmos missile website, the Indian Hewlett Packard helpdesk, the Indian Institute of Science, and the Indian Directorate General of Shipping. On December 4, 2010, a group calling itself the Pakistan Cyber Army hacked the website of the Central Bureau of Investigation, India's top investigating agency. While these defacements are just extensions of the tensions dating back to Pakistan and India's independence from British rule in 1947, it shows the pursuit of cyber as a means to gain the initiative in influencing regional and global opinion. On November 26, 2010, the Indian Cyber Army then hacked the Pakistan Army website and the websites of a number of Ministries including the Foreign Affairs, Education, and Finance. The attack was done as a revenge of the Mumbai terrorist attack which had confirmed the involvement of Pakistani terrorists.[75]

Based on these attacks and Pakistan's official website, it is now known that the Pakistan Cyber Army, an official part of the Pakistan Army, will a play a stealth role in future war, starting

---

[74] A hacker is an expert at programming and solving problems with a computer but is more often a person who illegally gains access to and sometimes tampers with information in a computer system. From the Merriam Webster Dictionary Online, http://www.merriam-webster.com/dictionary/hacker, accessed April 9, 2012.

[75] The Express Tribune, "36 Government Sites Hacked by 'Indian Cyber Army'," *The Express Tribune Online*, November 30, 2010. http://tribune.com.pk/story/83967/36-government-websites-hacked-by-indian-cyber-army/ (accessed December 30, 2011.)

with hacking, espionage, and data theft.[76] It is apparent that both Pakistan and India are using their cyber capability as a means to employ force without involving their conventional military forces or threat of nuclear war. While these events are minor compared to the more unrestrained Russian attacks, it shows how it is difficult to muster political will to counter cyber attacks with traditional military force. Both nations possess formidable conventional militaries, but these capabilities are not seen as morally justifiable deterrents to cyber attacks. As has been seen, kinetic retaliation for cyber attacks is a rare and politically hazardous event, especially when the source is ambiguous and difficult to precisely target.

September of 2010 witnessed another example of cyber warfare. Stuxnet was a virus that specifically targeted the Siemens supervisory control and data acquisition (SCADA) systems used to control the equipment in Iranian nuclear facilities. It is thought that the specific target was the Natanz uranium enrichment facility.[77] Stuxnet enabled the attackers to essentially take control of the facility's centrifuges, increasing and decreasing the rotor speed until excessive vibrations destroyed them. While the vibrations did not cause the catastrophic damage of Turbine #2 in Russia, it destroyed up to two thousand centrifuges and delayed Iran's progress on the development of nuclear capabilities.

According to Ralph Langner, who first identified the virus' final target, the Stuxnet worm is the most advanced piece of malware ever discovered and significantly increases the profile of cyber warfare.[78] It contains four zero-day exploits, two stolen personal identification certificates,

---

[76] Pakistan Defence Website. "Top Ten Weapons of Pakistan," under "Pakistan's Cyber Army." http://www.defence.pk/forums/pakistan-strategic-forces/127546-top-10-future-weapons-pakistan-3.html (accessed February 3, 2012).

[77] Pascal Mallet. "AFP: Stuxnet worm brings cyber warfare out of virtual world." *Agence France-Presse*. October 1, 2010. http://www.google.com/hostednews/afp/article/ALeqM5hWP5Ga_K2k4oOosf Mz39JFifrDaQ?docId=CNG.0c3a53ff7267f11501a5b3dbd9567dbf.2d1. (accessed 31 January 2012).

[78] Ralph Langner, "Cracking Stuxnet: A 21st-Century Cyber Weapon," March, 2011. http://www.ted.com/talks/ralph_langner_cracking_stuxnet_a_21st_century_cyberweapon.html. (accessed January 30, 2012).

28

a revolutionary way of storing information so as to go undetected, and it included a number of ways to limit its effects to ensure it affected only the targeted facilities. [79]  It was the limitations, written into the code of the malware that revealed the intent of the Stuxnet's creators.  The virus's driver files used two valid signed certificates, one from RealTek Semiconductors and one from JMicron Technology, both located in Taiwan.  The use of these valid certificates tricked the systems into thinking the malware was trusted software from one of those two companies.  This showed researchers that Stuxnet's creators had significant resources. [80]

Every time a computer was infected it was instructed to "phone home" to report information about the machine.  This information included the typical computer identification information such as IP address and computer name, but Stuxnet also reported whether the Sieman's Simatic Win CC Step 7 software was installed.  The computers with Step 7, as it was commonly called, were consolidated in Iran.  This was an anomaly in how most malware infections occur.  Usually the United States leads in the number of worldwide infections due to its high number of internet-connected computers, as compared to a country like Iran that has significantly fewer computers and connections.  Peeling back Stuxnet's onion of subprograms, it was discovered that it used a vulnerability in Step 7 to infect a server that could then infect more Step 7 machines.  "The attackers were ruthlessly spreading their malware, but in a strangely limited way." [81]

---

[79] A zero-day exploit is malware used to exploit vulnerabilities in software that are not yet known know to the software developer or anti-virus developers.  Out of the millions of malware detected each year, fewer than twelve are zero-day exploits.  The vast majority of malware is a variant of other known malware.  For more information on zero-day exploits see Tony Bradley, "Zero Day Exploits," November 11, 2011. http://netsecurity.about.com/od/newsandeditorial1/a/aazeroday.htm, (accessed April 3, 2012).

[80] Zetter, "How Digital Detectives Deciphered Stuxnet."

[81] Ibid.

29

A further limitation was uncovered in Stuxnet's configuration file. [82] Researchers found an end-date of June 24, 2012. Stuxnet would, as it infected each computer, check the machine's clock. If it was later than the June 2012 date then Stuxnet would cease operating. [83] In this way programmers could devise a fire and forget weapon that had an end date, when it would no longer pose a threat to other systems. Obviously, an unscrupulous designer could create malware that is unlimited in its duration.

The most dangerous part of Stuxnet was that it would intercept commands in the Step 7 software and replace them with its own commands. While this would normally set off an alarm at the server, Stuxnet specifically disabled the automated alarms. In this case, since sufficient intelligence existed on the computer defenses at Natanz, the designers of the malware designed a camouflage that allowed the malware to protect itself by transmitting false negatives that nothing was amiss. Researchers realized that Stuxnet was not designed for espionage, but for physical sabotage and they were alarmed. [84]

In piecing together what equipment was to be sabotaged, researchers took three weeks to determine what type of facility Stuxnet sought – an Iranian nuclear facility. Reverse engineering the code over months, researchers led by Liam O'Murchu of Symantec's California office discovered the technical configurations specifically reset the cycle spin rates for the centrifuges essential to the enrichment of uranium, but only at facilities that housed groupings of 164

---

[82] A configuration file is a file that contains data about a specific user, program, computer or file. A programmer uses it to control every aspect of the code such as how long it will spread and how long each exploit should work. For further information see PC Magazine's definition at http://www.pcmag.com/encyclopedia_term/0,2542,t=configuration+file&i=40232,00.asp (accessed April 3, 2012).

[83] Gregg Keizer, "Stuxnet Code Hints at Possible Israeli Origin," September 30, 2010, *Computer World*. http://www.computerworld.com/s/article/9188982/Stuxnet_code_hints_at_possible_Israeli_origin_researchers_say (accessed April 3, 2012).

[84] Zetter, "How Digital Detectives Deciphered Stuxnet."

centrifuges.[85] It would speed up the spin rate beyond its designed threshold, wait twenty seven days, then slow the spin rate to nearly stationary for fifty minutes, and then set the rate back to normal.[86] During the time of Stuxnet's greatest activity, inspectors from the Institute for Science and International Security noted that the Natanz Nuclear Enrichment Facility had approximately 1800 centrifuges replaced.[87] It was much later that these inspectors helped researchers discover that the Natanz plant was configured in groups of 164 centrifuges.[88]

The complexity and physical destruction by Stuxnet caused the world to take notice of the potentials of cyber war. Whereas malware up to that point mostly involved criminal activity or espionage, this was the first incident that was globally discussed by the best cyber researchers in the world. The fact that it used two stolen certificates, four zero day attacks, had limitations embedded, and focused on such a high value target as a nuclear facility caused the rest of the world realize the level of resources and commitment that were required for a successful strike.[89]

Stuxnet is significant for a variety of different reasons, but by far and away what is most significant about Stuxnet is that it achieved a kinetic effect, destroying strategic equipment, without traditional kinetic weaponry. This occurred while a significant public debate has taken

---

[85] Liam O'Murchu was joined by Eric Chien, technical director of Symantec Security Response, and Nicholas Falliere, a senior software engineer and code analyst in Symantec's Paris office. It was later that German Ralph Langier asserted that Stuxnet was targeting Iranian nuclear sites. From Zetter, "How Digital Detectives Deciphered Stuxnet."

[86] For more specific details on how the centrifuges were affected see David Albright and Andrea Stricker, "Stuxnet Worm Targets Automated Systems for Frequency Converters: Are Iranian Centrifuges the Target?" *Institute for Science and International Security*, December 20, 2010," http://isis-online.org/isis-reports/detail/stuxnet-worm-targets-automated-systems-for-frequency-converters-is-irans-ce/8, (accessed December 31, 2011).

[87] Kim Zetter, "Clues Suggest Stuxnet Virus Was Built for Subtle Nuclear Sabotage," *Wired*, November 15, 2010, under "Stuxnet" http://www.wired.com/threatlevel/2010/11/stuxnet-clues/ (accessed December 31, 2011).

[88] David Albright, Paul Brannan, and Christina Walrond, "Stuxnet Malware and Natanz: Update of ISIS December 22, 2010 Report." *Institute for Science and International Security*, February 15, 2011," http://isis-online.org/isis-reports/detail/stuxnet-malware-and-natanz-update-of-isis-december-22-2010-reportsupa-href1/ (accessed December 31, 2011).

[89] Zetter, "How Digital Detectives Deciphered Stuxnet."

place on the value of Israeli or US bombing strikes to destroy Iranian nuclear capabilities. Rather than a 1,000 pound bomb, a hundred year old piece of technology using chemical energy and fragmentation to destroy a piece of equipment, the virus commanded the equipment to destroy itself. The virus then was able to hide itself, pursuing a veil of anonymity. By searching through the Iranian nuclear network, the virus identified the centrifuges with pinpoint accuracy, at a time when it was debatable whether traditional visual means, such as human intelligence, spy satellites, drone aircraft, and manned bombers, could identify the target. This cyber attack once more demonstrated "the megabyte could always get through" to destroy a target that other means could not identify, let alone strike. Not only could it get through, it could find the target when no planner could see or identify the target's physical location. It used the computer's internal systems to let the target identify its location and then commanded it to destroy itself. It was a expert performance by an agency that is still unknown, unable to be counterattacked in a politically acceptable means, and difficult to deter or defend against. Stuxnet represented a new achievement in weaponization, and achieved the effect of a strategic bombing strike (the widely pronounced alternative) using wholly different means to achieve similar ends.

## Strategic Cyber Power - Near-Peer Competitor[90]

> Economic globalization and world multi-polarization are gaining momentum....The rise and decline of international strategic forces is quickening...new emerging powers are arising. Therefore, a profound readjustment is brewing in the international system.
> —*China's National Defense in 2008*[91]

---

[90] For a state to be a peer, it must have more than a strong military. Its power must be multidimensional—economic, technological, intellectual, etc.—and it must be capable of harnessing these capabilities to achieve a policy goal. To be a true peer, it has to be capable of challenging the hegemon on a global scale (and wish to do so), and the outcome of that challenge has to be uncertain, even if the hegemon effectively marshals its assets. From Thomas S. Szayna, et al., *The Emergence of Peer Competitors: A Framework for Analysis* (Washington, DC: The Rand Arroyo Center, 2001), 6.

[91] The People's Republic of China, *China's National Defense in 2008.* Beijing: Information Office of the State Council of the People's Republic of China, http://www.china.org.cn/government/whitepaper/node_7060059.htm (accessed January 12, 2012), 3.

The closest competitor to the United States for cyber superiority is the People's Republic of China, where there is great perceived demand for cutting age weaponry that is cheap and difficult to defend against. Through a focused strategy of information dominance and stealth, their systematic method of gaining cyber superiority has expanded from a local, shore-based operation to one that operates through the global commons of cyberspace, including the coastal shores of the American industrial base, the Pentagon, as well as critical infrastructure and banking hubs. Their government is currently looking to gain superiority over its near peer competitors, specifically the United States. As an aspiring economic leader, it seeks to gain power at the expense of nations such as the United States. The launching of their first aircraft carrier in 2010 and current developments and increases in missile capability will enable China to become a dominant force in the Pacific region.[92] However, much of the technology that these systems were built on was based on over a decade of systematic cyber infiltration into the industrial base of other nations. The government has maximized its ability to exploit cyber technology to spy on rival industry, and has cut corners in its drive to build military capacity. It seems likely as this technology becomes increasingly weaponized that the Chinese would take advantage of these asymmetric capabilities.

The Chinese military's demand for cyber capabilities has been a reality for several years. Their military has a fraction of the US defense budget, and is incapable of meeting American defense expenditures in traditional weapon systems. The government has placed more economic effort into their industrial base and construction of factories as they compete globally. Cyber capabilities allow the Chinese to circumvent their shortcomings in traditional military technology in much the same way that airpower allowed the United States to circumvent a large standing army to be attritted in bloody trench warfare. The growth of information technology in China has

---

[92] Andrew F. Krepinevich, "The Way to Respond to China," *The Los Angeles Times*, (November 9, 2011), http://articles.latimes.com/2011/nov/09/opinion/la-oe-krepinevich-pacific-20111109 (accessed April 3, 2012).

contributed to the infrastructure, enabled their government and businesses to learn from the

technologies developed by others, and increased the future role of information systems nation-

wide. As China looked to expand their internet and technological capabilities, their military did

likewise. Military leaders looked to the successes of the American forces in the 1990-1991

Persian Gulf War and sought ways to emulate them. But Chinese theorists also looked at how to

defeat what the Chinese call an "informatized" force.[93] They realized that an early-strike

offensive capability was as important, if not more important, than the ability to share intelligence

and communicate internally.[94]

Chinese military leaders recognized the power of focused attacks on key nodes as early as

2003. They developed doctrine where the military would attack multiple nodes, focusing on the

enemy's critical nodes followed by redundant nodes in order to maximize recovery time. The

interval between attacks would allow them to orient and observe the system, identifying weak

points through a series of nonkinetic cyber attacks and probes.[95] To be fair, this attacking of the

critical node is a reflection of airpower theory. It should come as no surprise that one of the

greatest early examples of this, a cyber attack against the Iraqi air defense computer system, was

in support of the coalition aerial offensive prior to Operation Desert Storm. Nevertheless, the

Chinese emulation and copying of American military doctrine shows an adaptability that must be

considered. Their ability to replicate an aerial bomber offensive with pinpoint strikes against key

nodes is demonstrating the similarities between these different means of attack.

---

[93] Chinese documents refer to both" informatized warfare" and "informationized warfare." They both come from their concept of information warfare. The concept of using information to gain dominance extends to other major areas, especially their national economic goals.

[94] Brian Krekel, "Capability of the People's Republic of China to Conduct Cyber Warfare and Computer Network Exploitation." Paper prepared for the U.S.-China Economic and Security Review Commission, Washington, DC (October 22, 2009) http://www.uscc.gov /researchpapers/2009/ NorthropGrumman_PRC_ Cyber_ paper_FINAL_Approved%20 Report_16Oct2009.pdf (accessed December 28, 2011).

[95] Shen Yongjun and Su Ruozhou, "PLA Sets to Push Forward Informationalization Drive from Three Aspects," *PLA Daily Online*, January 11, 2006. http://english.chinamil.com.cn/site2/news-channels/2006-01/11/content_382378.htm (accessed December 31, 2011).

The Chinese government has cautiously embraced technological development within its own borders. While it attempts to control and have overwatch on all commercial endeavors, including foreign investment, it also encourages embracing that technology to further national goals both internally and externally. It strikes a tenuous balance between nationalistic growth and the influence of outside factors.[96] Their investment in information technology education and the communications sector is not only paying economic dividends. Their army is leveraging their information technology workforce to man their information warfare militias, in some cases creating them directly within commercial firms.[97] The army also has an ever increasing number of firms capable of engineering and building advanced information warfare systems in support of their requirements. A tight linkage between aviation companies such as Boeing, North American, and Grumman was vital to focus industry in support of national aims. Where they have not built a capacity, the army has co-opted it or acquired it. There are thousands of known Chinese hackers active in the international community. Like elsewhere in the world, many are members of hacker groups and participate in developing malware and bypassing security measures.[98] There is evidence that the government openly supported hacker groups from 1999 to 2001. For example, after the 1999 bombing of the Chinese embassy in Serbia, government sponsored hackers mounted large scale attacks on the websites of multiple western countries to include the United States. The hacker group Javaphile was praised by the government for its successful hacking and defacement of the White House website.[99] However by 2001, in an about face, the same government issued statements discouraging such activities and highlighting that

---

[96] Krekel, "Capability of the People's Republic of China to Conduct Cyber Warfare and Computer Network Exploitation," 6.

[97] Ibid, 27.

[98] Short for "malicious software," malware refers to software programs designed to damage or do other unwanted actions on a computer system.

[99] Scott Henderson, *The Dark Visitor: Inside the World of Chinese Hackers* (Baltimore, MD: Henderson, 2007), 71.

such activities in any country were not to be tolerated.[100]  In February of 2009, the National

People's Congress expanded their anti-hacking law to include criminalizing the dissemination of

malicious software.  Previous laws only prohibited the hacking of their own government systems

and left wide latitude for cyber criminals. [101]

In January of 2010, cyber activities drew global attention when Google shut down

operations in China after claiming its server were being attacked from within.[102]  Following these

allegations, the government issued statements that their highest courts were addressing how

hacking crimes should be handled by the courts.[103]  These attacks were eventually traced back to

two universities, Shanghai Jiaotong University and the Lanxiang Vocational School.  Jiaotong

University has one of China's top computer science programs and in 2009, its students won the

"Battle of the Brains" international computer programming competition sponsored by I.B.M.,

beating out Stanford and other top-flight universities.  Lanxiang is a vocational school that was

established with military support and trains a large number of computer scientists for the

military.[104]  There is, of course, no equivalent school in the United States.  The most interesting

piece of this incident was that Google acknowledged that they censored the search results at the

---

[100] Vivien Pik-kwan Chan, "HK: SCMP Report on PRC Officials Condemning Hacker Attacks," *Hong Kong South China Morning Post*, 8 May 01.

[101] Owen Fletcher, "China Denies Cyber Spy Network Charges," *PC World*, Mar 31, 2009, http://www.pcworld.com/article/162270/china_denies_cyber_spy_network_charges.html, (accessed January 1, 2012).

[102] Kim Zetter, "Google Hack Attack Was Ultra Sophisticated, New Details Show." *Wired*. January 14, 2010.  http://www.wired.com/threatlevel/2010/01/operation-aurora/ (accessed December 30, 2011).

[103] Owen Fletcher, "China Takes Step to Toughen Hacking Laws," *Computerworld*, February 2, 2010.  http://www.computerworld.com/s/article/9150718/China_takes_step_to_toughen_hacking_laws (accessed  January 1, 2012).

[104] John Markoff and David Barbosa, "Two China Schools Said to be Tied to Online Attacks." *The New York Times*. February 18, 2010.  http://www.nytimes.com/2010/02/19/technology/19china.html, (accessed January 2, 2012).

request of the Chinese government.[105] This censorship was another way the government co-opted companies, in this case an American one, into executing its information warfare strategy. There are similarities between the government encouraged creativity directed toward these hackers, and the heyday of aviation growth of the Interwar period, where much of the technological benefits found their way to military applications.

Like the airpower theorists and the conflicts they faced in the interwar period, the Chinese development of cyber capabilities have faced challenges in the competition for funding and resources from other, more traditional sources of combat power. The government has prioritized their core strength of a large standing army, based on their immense pools of manpower, but this is not a global threat as they lack the assets to project this power beyond their mainland to the global stage. The sorts of power projection that the Chinese military would need are prohibitively expensive and reside in areas they have little expertise in. For example, it has never had a blue water navy, and lacks a doctrine or tradition on how to employ such a force. Similarly, its air force would require large budget to have the remotest chance of competing with the United States Air Force. The Chinese government has decided not to compete in such pointless endeavors. As a result, the stature of their traditional forces is threatened by efforts to expand disruptive measures such as the cyber efforts. These have the potential to apply pressure to compel us to bend to Chinese will at a fraction of the expenditure a traditional effort would require. The Chinese defense budget is estimated by many sources at no greater than one third of America's budget. With the exception of raw manpower, they are qualitative and quantitatively outclassed in many traditional weapon systems, such as tanks, aircraft, submarines, and ships. There is great incentive for them to search for an asymmetrical advantage in a domain where the

---

[105] Kim Zetter, "Google to Stop Censoring Search Results in China After Hack Attack," *Wired*, January 12, 2010. http://www.wired.com/threatlevel/2010/01/google-censorship-china/, (accessed December 30, 2011).

United States government can be outmaneuvered and outspent. As a result, the Chinese are supporting cyber warfare as a greater fraction of their budget.

Like the US Army Air Corps, inspirational and visionary leaders have had great impact on the Chinese cyber forces. In 1995 General Wang Pufeng, who is considered the father of the Chinese doctrine of information warfare, proffered that the goal of information warfare is no longer the conquest of territory or the destruction of the enemy's army, but destruction of the enemy's will to resist.[106] Like Douhet, who saw the power of aviation as a means to strike at popular will, Pufeng saw the power of information warfare to strike at the will of the people as a way to win future wars. It is worth observing that while Pufeng saw the goal of information warfare not as destruction of an enemy army, this insight may have been rendered less relevant with the weaponization of cyber. Pufeng's thoughts can be interpreted less as restraint than an admission of the limits of contemporary technology. As those limits are wiped away, Chinese intentions can approach a less restrained doctrine. Chinese cyber theorists resonate Sun Tzu and see cyber warfare as a means to subdue the enemy without battle.[107] General Pufeng also suggests that in a "people's war" civilian and military experts could be united in the same goal.[108] Also in 1995, Colonel Wang Baocun and Li Fei stated that the purpose of cyber warfare is to "force the enemy side to regard their goal as our goal," to "force the opponent to give up the will to resist and end the confrontation and stop fighting by attacking an enemy's perception and belief via information energy."[109] Four years later, Qiao Liang and Wang Xiangsui in their book

---

[106] Major General Wang Pufeng, "The Challenge of Information Warfare" (1995), reproduced in *Chinese Views of Future Warfare*, National Defense University, online at http://www.au.af.mil/au/awc/awcgate/ndu/chinview/chinacont.html (accessed December 24, 2011).

[107] Samuel B. Griffith,, ed. and trans. *Sun Tzu: The Art of War*. (New York: Oxford University Press, 1971), 39. This was derived from "Thus without battle his army was conquered, his cities taken; and his state overthrown."

[108] Daniel Ventre, *Information Warfare* (London: ISTE Ltd, 2009), 56

[109] Colonels Wang Baocun and Li Fei, "Information Warfare," *People's Liberation Army Daily*, June 20, 1995 http://www.fas.org/irp/world/china/docs/iw_wang.htm (accessed December 26, 2011).

*Unrestricted Warfare* highlighted that …technological progress has given us the means to strike at the enemy's nerve centre directly without harming other things, giving us numerous new options for achieving victory, and all these make people believe that the best way to achieve victory is to control not to kill.[110]

The two Chinese colonels go on to define "unrestricted warfare" as a condition where "weapons and techniques are now multiple and that the battlefield is now everywhere." In short, "there is no longer any distinction between what is or is not the battlefield."[111] It is curious that an underlying assumption of this statement is that there used to be such a distinction. Writers such as Douhet chose to deny such a distinction when they advocated strategic bombing of civilian targets. If there has not been a distinction between what is or is not the battlefield, then the new doctrine points to less a distinction in what is a target then in the permissible means to strike them. Colonels Liang and Ziangsui highlight that destruction is not necessarily desired in future war; "technical progress offers many new possibilities of conquering. And this makes us think that the best way to be victorious is to control and not to kill."[112] Students compete for entrance to the highly competitive and prestigious Peking University (also known as Beijing University) and Tsinghua Universities. These universities are universally heralded as the Harvard and MIT of China. The information technology workforce in Beijing is approximately one million people and is expected to grow further as the Chinese government continues to improve their education system.[113] Beijing is the home to the prestigious Peking University. While the Chinese government uses these universities for research, there is no evidence that they tap the

---

[110] Qiao Liang and Wang Xiangsui, *Unrestricted Warfare* (Beijing: PLA Literature and Arts Publishing House, 1999), 18

[111] Ibid., 141.

[112] Ventre, *Information Warfare*, 59.

[113] This is as of December 2010 according to Global Outsourcing conference website. http://www.globalservicesmedia.com/Destinations/China/Beijing:The-Birthplace-of-China's-IT-Industry/25/21/10291/GS101217969024 , accessed on December 24, 2011.

student talent until after they enter the work force. The United States, in contrast, has no such recruiting drive for cyber professionals tied to the Department of Defense. In feeder communities, such as the Signal Corps or Military Intelligence fields, ones choice of undergraduate degree is irrelevant to branch selection.

It is difficult to compare these universities with American military schools, but we must again look back to the rise of airpower and acknowledge that a common educational base that frames a common vision for the community is an essential aspect of organizational growth. The Chinese have mobilized students by mandating that selected individuals attend technical universities to study government-directed courses. The large number of Chinese educated in these schools dwarfs that of the American cyber community (which has no equivalent) and bears a strong resemblance to Maxwell Field, where the fledgling American aviation community developed its unique approach to war. The fact that the Chinese have developed an organized education and doctrinal core to their approach to cyber warfare stands in comparison to the US aviation community of the 1930s, and leaves the present day American cyber community far behind. The American cyber community is disorganized; lacking a doctrinal center of excellence there is no shared vision of where the community is or should be going. Lacking a shared vision means that as technological breakthroughs are made, budgets, resources, and command emphasis will be frittered away on less successful and lucrative programs.

China's economic development strategy goes beyond its educational reform. Their government has also invested heavily in its communication infrastructure and provided a legal framework and economic incentives for the labor and financial markets.[114] While this reads well in the international arena of investments and banking, there is still some lingering skepticism of Chinese intentions. The opening of their markets could bring in the investments and

---

[114] Carl J. Dahlman and Jean-Eric Aubert, *China and the Knowledge Economy: Seizing the 21st Century*, WBI Development Studies, (Washington, DC: The World Bank, 2002), 49.

technological developments from the rest of the world, but also note that may threaten the sovereignty of their government. The Chinese government has carefully and patiently managed the last thirty-four years of economic reform under the Four Modernization and is keenly aware of the influences other cultures could have on their own.[115]

China's position as a competitor with the United States has elevated the importance of a cyber capability, and contributed to the rise of their growth. The China's People Liberation Army is a keen observer of American military operations, using lessons learned to supplement and update Chinese strategic thought and planning. This has been particularly true with US operations in the first decade of this century, specifically Operation Iraqi Freedom and Operation Enduring Freedom. One of the key PLA lessons learned from these operations is the centrality of information on the battlefield and the impact of attacking key nodes rather than across a broad front of activity.[116] Earlier military events, such as the US cyber attack against Iraqi Air Defense computers during the onset of Operation Desert Storm, have not gone unnoticed.

Parallels between this Chinese doctrine and the rise of American airpower are apparent in regard to doctrinal development. The Chinese are analyzing information warfare as a possible substitute for conventional, traditional combat systems because it is relatively cheap and able to more effectively attack the enemy will. The creative ability to recognize a new weapon system, and define the battlefield to be nearly everywhere, resonated with the airpower theorists and their efforts to expand the battlefield, to include the enemy's cities and make any location a potential target for aerial attack. By targeting the population centers, they destroy public will and support for the conflict. The Chinese government can then achieve their political goals without

---

[115] The Four Modernizations The Four Modernizations were goals to strengthen the fields of agriculture, industry, national defense, science and technology in China. The Four Modernizations were adopted as a means of rejuvenating China's economy in 1978 by Deng Xiaoping following the death of Mao Zedong.

[116] Dr. Eric C. Anderson and Jeffrey G. Engstrom. "Capabilities of the Chinese People's Liberation Army to Carryout Military Action in the Event of a Regional Military Conflict." Paper prepared for the U.S.-China Economic and Security Review Commission. SAIC, March 2009.

significant losses of life or resources. Equally importantly, they can build an asymmetric strategic capability that is both cheap and immune from the countermeasures of a largely traditional US military machine. Axis powers such as Germany and Japan focused on land and sea power because those were the decisive sources of power in World War I and the interwar period. Today we recognize, in hindsight, that airpower theorists were correct in their appraisal of airpower's future capability. Today the Chinese realize that cyber warfare could be the next weapon to bypass traditional combat power to destroy enemy willpower. It could be an unrecoverable mistake if the American government were to allow them to gain such a strategic advantage.

Cyber organizations in the United States must also look at the systematic way in which Chinese cyber capability has grown. Airpower was of little interest to military leaders until it showed a weaponized capability. The Chinese were not the first to develop or foresee the use of cyber capability; these writings, published in 1995, postdate American usage in Operation Desert Storm. Yet the Chinese showed parallels with the US Army Air Corps during the interwar period by developing a doctrinal base. Without possessing the ability to carry out an attack, Chinese theorists developed concepts and doctrine for their use. Similarly, American air theorists developed plans at Maxwell Field for use of a bomber that did not exist. In contrast, the US cyber community had a significant head start on the Chinese, yet has frittered it away through an inability to develop a theory of war that maximized the capability of cyber warfare. In contrast, the National Military Strategy consigns cyber warfare to a supporting effort, conceptually similar to the supporting effort of the tactically oriented, and strategically ineffective, German Luftwaffe. As an example, this strategy states that "Cyberspace capabilities enable Combatant Commanders to operate effectively across all domains."[117] Our military strategists see cyber capabilities as

---

[117] Chairman, Joint Chiefs of Staff, *The National Military Strategy of the United States of America, 2011: Redefining America's Military Leadership* (Washington, DC: Government Printing Office, 2011), 10.

supporting efforts to enable traditional capabilities. This strategy does not maximize the potential of this new weapon, or consider the deterrence effect of resourcing offensive capabilities.

It was within these contexts that the Chinese military organized to achieve advantage through informatization. Information warfare emerged in their defense doctrine in the early 2000's with the defined goal of fighting "Local Wars Under Informationized Conditions" that seeks to develop a fully networked architecture capable of coordinating military operations on land, in the air, at sea, in space and across the electromagnetic spectrum.[118] In these aspects, the Chinese followed the American military's lead in network-centric warfare.

However, in the offensive capability, the "Integrated Network Electronic Warfare" authored by then-Colonel Dai Qingmin in 1995, appeared to be ahead of American theorists. Qingmin's work integrated electronic warfare, computer network attack, computer network defense, and intelligence operations through computer network exploitation. The joint action of network attack and electronic warfare against the networks, mission command nodes, intelligence capabilities, logistics systems, infrastructure, targeting systems, corporations, industry leaders, and technological innovators of their foes and competitors constitutes the basis of offensive Chinese cyber warfare and sets them apart from many of their peers.[119]

The Chinese Army organized its Third and Fourth General Staff Department's around its defensive and offensive strategies, respectively. The Third Department (Signals Intelligence) is responsible for computer network defense and intelligence gathering. The Fourth Department (Electronic Countermeasures) has the offensive mission for both computer network attack and electronic warfare. The selection of Major General Dai Qingmin as the director of this department informed the international community that his offensive view of cyber warfare was an

---

[118] Krekel, "Capability of the People's Republic of China to Conduct Cyber Warfare and Computer Network Exploitation," 10.

[119] Ibid., 13-14.

accepted strategy for the Chinese Army.  In fact, in 2000 General Dai broke with military tradition and advocated for pre-emptive cyber attacks to gain the initiative.[120]  Colonel Wang Baocun sees information warfare as "a form of combat action...that involves military security, deception, physical attack, electronic warfare, psychological warfare and netwar."[121]

General Dai's doctrine of the offensive has echoed the early airpower theorists.  His idea of the first offensive, and an acceptance of the need for a first strike in the cyber arena demonstrates the understanding that the cyber attack will always get through, and that preemptive strikes are stronger because the first effective strike will not be able to be countered. A lack of cyber deterrence through an offensive focus and attack capability prompts rival nations to build a capability of their own.  The world's best army, navy, and air force do not deter cyber attacks; in fact they attract an asymmetric response.  Current American defense expenditures, tied to a significant policy and budgetary cyber shortfall, draws attention to such an Achilles heel.  Similarly, an army of the 1940's that did not have the benefits of friendly air superiority was decisively disadvantaged.

The German theorist Karl Von Clausewitz wrote that defense is the stronger form of war, yet unique technologies that cannot be countered turn this theory on its head.[122]  Airpower theorists wrote that the bomber could always get through, and advocated an offense-centric strategy.  While casualties were higher than anticipated, airpower contributed greatly to the destruction of Nazi Germany and broke Japanese resistance.  More pertinently, "mutually assured destruction" was a deterrence based strategy where the ability of a nation to prevent or withstand a nuclear strike was nonexistent. The Soviet Union built a deterrence strategy through a stockpile

---

[120] Timothy L. Thomas, "China's Electronic Strategies," *Military Review*, (May-June 2001), 47.

[121] Wang Baocun, "The Current Revolution in Military Affair and its Impact on the Asia-Pacific Region," *China Military Science Review*, (April 2000), 138.

[122] Roger T. Ames, trans. *Sun Tzu: The Art of Warfare* (NY: Ballantine, 1993), 115.

of offensive weapons, which were never used but prevented the inclination of the other power to employ theirs, for fear of a counterattack.[123]

Today the American cyber strategy is amateurish and incomprehensible. Knowing the inability to prevent the megabyte, like the bomber, from getting through, the cyber community has adopted a strategically unsound defensive posture that has been proven to be ineffective, while their largest competitor adopts an offensive strategy. Technological progress indicates that the United States government cannot overcome offensive capabilities of the Chinese; and a lack of a deterrence capability gives the Chinese no good reason not to employ these weapons.

A possible analogy where one side produced an offensive capability, where another pursued a defensive capability that was unproven and unsound, would be the 1940 French obsession with using the Maginot Line to defend against the German blitzkrieg. Following the end of World War I, German theorists developed the theory of lightning war, or blitzkrieg. They believed fast moving tanks and bombers could create an unstoppable offensive capability. In contrast, the French believed little had changed since World War I and even stronger defensive fortifications, like the World War I trenches, would dominate the battlefield.[124] Significantly, the decision makers who put all of their eggs in the basket of the strategic defense were not knowledgeable members of the armored community, and they adopted these courses of action in spite of, rather than alongside of, those with the most expertise, such as those of the French General De Gaulle who warned against an overwhelming German mechanical force smashing through French defenses.[125] The French possessed tanks in sufficient numbers, yet poor doctrine, strategy, and leadership frittered away this capability. What resulted in 1940 was a force that was defensive, and reactive in nature, believing that they could weather the blows of an attacker and

---

[123] Freedman, *Deterrence*, 9.

[124] Alistair Horne, *To Lose a Battle: France 1940* (London, UK: Penguin Books, 1969), 71.

[125] Ibid., 226.

survive, and a rival power that deduced, correctly, that a change in the balance of power had made the tank and the armored division able to defeat the best laid plans of the defender.[126] An unbalanced defensive mindset, that refused to build a balanced offensive capability, failed to gain success in 1940 armored warfare; it may well fail to do so in 2012 cyber warfare.

There are many similarities between the French strategic mistakes prior to the blitzkrieg against the Maginot line in 1940, and the direction cyber may be heading. The French anticipated the Germans would attack and that they could prepare for it and successfully defend against it. The Germans attacked in a way the French didn't anticipate, and it was catastrophically successful. The French anticipated the Germans would use the WWI Schlieffen Plan with a strong right flank so the French intended to use the line to canalize the German attack.[127] When the Germans penetrated the gap between the line and the troops the French had on the left, they broke through. The French thought they knew how the Germans would act, but then the Germans didn't do what they expected.

The French made numerous planning errors in the interwar construction of their line. Rather than adopt a balanced or an offensive strategy, or deter the German tanks with French tanks, the French tried to be strong everywhere. They assumed the defense is stronger than the offense, because those were the lessons of the last war, World War I. They believed these lessons would predict the results of the future one. The French planners conceded the initiative to Germans, and importantly, underestimated the truism that defending everywhere is expensive...budget overruns compromised their defensive schemes, and they ran short of funding in the middle of construction.[128] Weak points in the defenses were detected by the Germans at Sedan, twenty miles west of where the Maginot line ended. They used the initiative to defeat the

---

[126] Robert A. Doughty, *The Breaking Point: Sedan and the Fall of France, 1940* ( Hamdon, CT: Archon, 1990), 5.

[127] Ibid., 11.

[128] Horne, *To Lose a Battle: France 1940*, 74.

French at the decisive point. The French made human errors that compounded the problem; they attacked with their maneuver forces into Belgium and were outflanked in turn.[129] We can predict a cyber equivalent to a Maginot would have similar negative outcomes. The American cyberspace cannot be strong everywhere; the government and business cannot afford such a defense. We can build a defense, and it will in all likelihood work as advertised and defend key points, as did the Maginot Line, but we cannot be strong everywhere, or afford to defend everything. Enemy attackers will find weak points in our cyber defenses and be encouraged to attack by a lack of a credible, balanced response. It is possible to deter an enemy attack with a similar capability, and strategists can realize, and understand, that the lessons of last wars may do little to predict the future. The French did not have a clear doctrine or concept for using armor in mass, like the Germans. When they lost the initiative, they could not regain it. An excessive reliance on defense, vice balance, resulted in a loss of flexibility, and a lack of options that turned a tactical defeat at Sedan into a strategic catastrophe. Amazingly, in 1938 the French conducted exercises that indicated their strategy would fail. The results were suppressed, less they cause morale to suffer. "The result was a defeat so comprehensive a nature that the wisdom of publishing it was questioned lest morale be damaged."[130] Today, we see indications that cyber defenses will fail before a determined attack, and carry on regardless. The American cyber community also must observe its future competitors, understand their doctrine, and anticipate how they will use it against them.

Today, the Chinese openly advocate an offensive cyber-blitzkrieg approach. The US cyber community has excellent technical capabilities and excellent cyber operators hampered by a defensive doctrine, lack of centralized employment, and muddled strategic thinking. As long as

---

[129] Ibid., 139.

[130] Martin Marix Evans, *The Fall of France: Act with Daring* (Oxford, UK: Osprey Publishing, 2000), 48.

the US government refuses to organize, adopts a deterrence strategy, and chooses to concede the initiative to a Chinese first strike, all of the American eggs are placed in the theoretical basket that they can withstand a cyber strike. There is no evidence that this is possible; the history of cyber warfare, like that of airpower, nuclear deterrence theory, and the blitzkrieg, is that attacking first is the only viable option and deterrent. It is understandable that US doctrine would be faulty; unlike the Army Air Corps, there is no Maxwell Field, no doctrinal clearing house, and no location where the best minds in this field can meet and debate such ideas. Like the French, the Department of Defense has excellent equipment, to rival their armor. It does not have excellent doctrine or vision; and lacks an offensive capability. The United States would be challenged to deter or counterattack an enemy cyber strike. It encourages an enemy first strike; and concedes the initiative and options if the enemy strike is successful. The history of attacks in Estonia and Georgia lead us to believe defending against an attack is a great challenge; the history of the Maginot line also points to the inescapable fact that money when in short supply, creates gaps in coverage and defenses.[131] It was easier for the Germans to identify one weak point than for the French to create a defense with no weak points. It is easier for a rival to find a gap in the defenses of our national computer infrastructure than it is for us to defend everywhere on a limited budget. We can conclude, that unlike the French, an offensive, deterrence based strategy would be more successful. The current strategy has no chance of success at all.

Psychologically, deterrence has best been appreciated when it deters a capability that uses similar means. Prior to the start of World War I naval power was a key competitive issue between Germany and Great Britain. Airpower theorists were experts in their fields, and advocated increasing expenditures in rival air fleets. Nuclear arms in the Cold War prompted greater arrays of Nuclear weapons, countermeasures such as "Star Wars", and competition to deter the potential of a nuclear strike. The nuclear triad, of air based delivery intercontinental

---

[131] Horne, *To Lose a Battle: France 1940*, 74.

ballistic missiles, and nuclear armed submarines, created the flexibility to deter Soviet nuclear advances. One can conclude that a muscle bound but inflexible traditional force, or even one that has unconventional capabilities post Iraq and Afghanistan will be poorly prepared to deter a disruptive cyber attack. The inherent advantages of American traditional capabilities, coupled with a disruptive relative disadvantage, invites attack and draws attention to our lack of cyber deterrence.

A lack of deterrence can be traced back to the American documents that define its military's cyber strategy. The National Security Strategy of 2010 defines cyber strategy strictly in defensive terms. It advocates that we must "protect against biological attacks and challenges to the cyber networks that we depend upon."[132] Later, it states that "The space and cyberspace capabilities that power our daily lives and military operations are vulnerable to disruption and attack."[133] It advocates that we should "be prepared for asymmetric threats, such as those that target our reliance on space and cyberspace."[134] On page 27, the strategy states that we must "secure" cyberspace, This two page reference to cyber uses words such as "secure", and "defending" and that the US should "deter, prevent, detect, defend against, and quickly recover from cyber intrusions and attacks."[135] In short, the National Security Strategy advocates a cyber Maginot Line. If the Security Strategy prefers a virtual Maginot Line, the National Defense Strategy of 2008 is worse. It refers to "cyber threats" as small groups or individuals that can "attack vulnerable points in cyberspace" and adversaries that can exploit "…cyber and other forms of warfare."[136] Interestingly, it admits that "…China is developing technologies to disrupt

---

[132] President, United States of America, *The National Security Strategy, May 2010* (Washington, DC: Government Printing Office, 2010), 4.

[133] Ibid., 8

[134] Ibid., 17

[135] Ibid., 27-28

[136] Chairman, Joint Chiefs of Staff, *The National Military Strategy of the United States of America, 2011: Redefining America's Military Leadership*, 1, 7 and 11.

our traditional advantages. Examples include development of anti-satellite capabilities and cyber warfare."[137] But then this strategy goes on to disregard cyber for the rest of the document.

A side by side examination of American and Chinese narratives indicates that, partly due to a lack of an intellectual or doctrinal clearing house, cyber has no voice; what voice it has is incoherent. The default setting for the US cyber community is to protect, and defend, while our enemies advocate strike and attack. This is approaching crisis level for a community where offense is inherently superior to defense.

In 2003, the China's Central Military Commission Committee endorsed a concept of "3 Warfares" that includes media warfare, psychological warfare, and legal warfare. Using information operations, the Chinese government will conduct operations to influence internal and external opinion in the global media context. An example of this is when Google accused China of hacking their servers for information and the British media stated that the attacks were traced back to two Chinese schools; the Chinese national media denied the report. Not only will the Chinese operate in secret and employ "clever methods" to conduct intelligence operations, they will then engage in a "divine manipulation of the threads" in order to present the picture of what they want the world to believe.[138]

The Chinese historically are defensive in nature. From the building of the Great Wall to World War II, the Chinese have not fought a war far from its territorial borders. Its influence beyond its borders during the Cold War saw it fight in close proximity to its homeland. Battling the US on the Korean peninsula and backing the North Vietnamese Communists enabled the Chinese to demonstrate their rise in power, while staying within their regional area. However

---

[137] Ibid., 22.

[138] General Niu Li stated it would be necessary to use "clever methods" to gain information supremacy and win information warfare at a relatively low cost in *Unrestricted Warfare*, 99 and Sun Tzu, A divine manipulation of the threads, deception operations in order to defeat enemies. Ames, *Sun Tzu: The Art of Warfare*, 168.

50

that strategic paradigm has clearly shifted. Cyberspace gives the Chinese people the ability to be offensive, projecting effects on the shores of other nations and entities, while still fighting from their own shores, a better fit for their strategic culture. Information warfare has a far greater range than rifles, ships, airplanes, or even missiles. With their current infrastructure, military capability, and culture China cannot mobilize the strength of its people unless an adversary invades. In cyber war, a computer and connectivity to the internet gives the people the ability to project effects outside China. This is similar to the ways in which airpower allowed the distant United States to project power through the air against targets in Europe and the Pacific. The information age will limit the number of people who can fight the "People's War," but that smaller number will be more educated, connected and thus have greater range. In such a scenario, future adversaries of China can expect the government to resource and synchronize the efforts of the people.[139]

There are multiple lessons to be learned from an analysis and examination of the Chinese cyber community. The first is that this should be cause for grave concern in the United States. In any measureable and objective way the expansion and potential of Chinese cyber infrastructure has surpassed that of the United States. The Chinese have a doctrine and a vision for offensive employment that is based on an understanding of the potential of cyber and the balance of power between offensive and defensive means. Based on their understanding of this balance they have allocated resources accordingly and appropriately. They have bypassed more traditional approaches to war in favor of one that the United States holds no inherent advantage in. They have furthermore made forward thinking decisions in pursuit of sound doctrine, recruiting, education and training, and funding. By all means their plans have proven successful thus far. We should, therefore, make the following conclusions: The model first presented in the growth of the USAAC was sound; the Chinese adoption of a similar model will probably bring them

---

[139] Henderson, *The Dark Visitor: Inside the World of Chinese Hackers*, 104.

positive results; under most circumstances this would serve as an excellent model for the US

Cyber community; given that it is demonstrated by a rival, peer competitor, and potential future

enemy, should be unsettling information to US planners. It is, therefore, both a spur, and a model

for future development.

## Conclusions

Before focusing on the conclusions that this monograph has derived from the work on

this paper, it is vital to begin with revisiting a planning assumption. US Army *Field Manual 5-0,*

*The Operations Process,* says an assumption is "a supposition on the current situation or a

presupposition on the future course of events, either or both assumed to be true in the absence of

positive proof."[140] Assumptions are likely to be true, and necessary, that is vital, to continue

planning. In this case, the assumption that is necessary is that cyber warfare is a facet of warfare

that will have increasing, vice decreasing influence on the future of war. It is not known if this is

factually true, or false. Technologies tomorrow may make modern industrial infrastructure

impervious to cyber attack. Defensive means may soon be cheaply obtainable and the ability to

strike and destroy using cyber may decrease to virtually zero. If so, then scarce resources spent

on cyber may be wasted resources. In 1913, it was impossible to forecast the future of aviation.

Today the US cyber community finds it difficult to chart the future of cyber warfare. To consider

through the prism of risk management, it is unclear whether a future cyber attack is likely, or

unlikely. Yet the results may very well be catastrophic. To ignore such a potential loss at may be

at the expense of Amercian government and economy. To recap, it is assumed cyber warfare will

increase, not decrease in importance. Its role in the defense community will rise, not fall. Like

other technologies that were once emerging but now a static, known part of the defense

community, such as airpower, submarines, intercontinental ballistic missiles, special operations,

---

[140] *FM 5-0 2010: The Planning Process* (Washington, D.C.: U.S. Department of the Army, 2010), 2-10.

to name a few, while our predecessors may have not always seen its future potential, marginalizing cyber is at our peril.

Thomas Kuhn discussed the use of a paradigm as "what members of a scientific community, and they alone, share."[141] Most members of the military community do not share a vision of cyber warfare as a decisive tool. They think about it only as a threat to "hack" data, if they regard it at all. This shared paradigm is hazardous if it stifles America's ability to compete with her competitors the Chinese, who share a completely different paradigm.

One of the stated goals of this paper is to chart a better future for the cyber community. In order to do so, it is important to first understand the situation, envision a better future, and lay out effective ways to bring it about. In this situation the environment has a small set of historical data points and an uncertain future. Recent events indicate that it is difficult to defend against a cyber attack. The national cyber community is disorganized, the continental infrastructure is vulnerable, and America's peer competitor has adopted an offensive doctrine that exploits our vulnerabilities. The United States is either entering a state of crisis, or in a high likelihood of approaching one. Given a lack of historical evidence, it is quite possible that if the American military were to enter such a state, experts would have limited ability to realize it, until it was too late.

The envisioned better future is one where this state of crisis is averted. Cyber warfare is, at a minimum, a medium where the United States has parity with peer competitors, at least to the degree that can deter enemy attacks. The best case is a medium where the American organizations have dominance, cyber superiority or cyber supremacy, similar to our current level of air supremacy in the air domain. In such a best case the capabilities of a future US joint cyber capability, like that of airpower in World War II, can make America less reliant on more

---

[141] Thomas Kuhn, *The Essential Tension: Selected Studies in Scientific Tradition and Change*, (Chicago, University of Chicago Press, 1977), xxli.

traditional organizations, and offer the potential for a cheaper, swifter victory. In the near future, the government must realize the potential for warfare in the cyber arena, at a minimum so that military and political leaders are cognizant of its potential.

Having laid out a better future with, best case, cyber supremacy, minimally cyber parity, the US government must lay out an effective way to bring this about. In short, there must be a plan. It will probably come as little surprise to the reader that this monograph considers the best way to bring this about, the best way to achieve this better future, is to look for a past success and follow that example. In this case the model of the rise of the United States Army Air Force will suffice.

The first recommended change is the organization. The US department of defense must organize, and do so rapidly. Organization in and of itself will not solve our problems but a disorganized cyber community is incapable of the unity of effort required. By the nature of the problem, CYBERCOM must be unified and joint; the service components must relinquish their manpower and these must contribute to a joint community where the shared vision of the vital need to fight and win in the cyber domain trumps service loyalties and parochialism. Moreover, personnel that enter the joint cyber community should be led and managed from within that community. A career path should have at its end a world class practitioner of this art. Much as the Army Air Corps learned, officers that have mixed loyalties will possess neither the expertise nor the experience to serve two masters and be competent in neither.

In looking at the "cyber community," several things should be acknowledged. Firstly, in the United States it is fragmented, and un-unified and this must be fixed. Cyber experts who are now parts of various disparate commands must unify. Based on our national strategy, which is in itself flawed, the bulk of the attention and budget stream focus on defensive means which are in themselves, fragmented, based on the specific defensive needs of each service. Some small subcommunities, such as the National Security Agency, may have some offensive capability, but it is obviously difficult to integrate such a view when many of the best and most intelligent

54

members of the community do not have the security clearances to participate in relevant discussions. This needs to be addressed, and solved.

The question of who belongs in the cyber community is relevant because of a key point: there is very little objective data to build a theory upon. There have been cyber attacks, of differing levels of severity, but in absence of large amounts of concrete evidence and discrete data points, fundamental questions that must be resolved, such as "is offense stronger than defense? Where should the budget focus?" "Will the Megabyte always get through?" will be in the realm of the theorist, vice the historian. It is easy to get these questions wrong. Theorists in the 1930s struggled to get them right in the Army Air Corps, and this was a community where there was no doubt who was in and not in aviation, and there were no walls of secrecy preventing open discourse. On the contrary, the growth of aviation was a public event open to all to see and observe. To answer such vitally important questions regarding the future of this new capability, as wide an area of expertise as possible needs to be canvassed. The high-tech communities that have expertise in these domains are largely civilian in population. The point is to understand that unlike the infantry, artillery, or attack aviation, the military does not hold a monopoly of expertise in this area and planners should not limit their research to a narrowly focused group.

The second step along this new way resides in doctrine. This author believes that radical steps are needed to thrive and succeed, but before questions are answered and problems are solved, the cyber community must ensure they asking the right questions. The Department of Defense needs to build Maxwell Field. The new Joint Cyber Command as envisioned must start with education. There must be a joint school, where these future leaders are educated and trained. The very best in the community must be selected to teach there. Unity of effort in this arena begins with a common view as to where the cyber community is and where it is going, and the Maxwell model is an outstanding example of this. What is the role of cyber, what weapons does it need? What is the road ahead? It is difficult to answer such questions, especially when it is uncertain who should be doing the answering. Therefore, we must have a school. We must select the elite to hold the keys to such an education, and all in the community who seek to make a difference must pass through it.

One of the first problems such a school should attack is to produce a vision for what such a war would look like. Is cyber warfare inherently offensive, as early airpower theorists believed, or, in the more traditional and Clauswitzian sense, is it defensive in nature? Should the United States government spend scarce resources attempting the historically unprecedented task of securing the nation from attack, or should they adopt the offensive strategy to seize the initiative, put the future potential enemy on the defensive, and in so doing, achieve deterrence? It is tempting to answer such a question now, but cyber theorists would do better at analyzing such problems if the department of defense built the organization, then built a school at the heart of the organization, and then used that to chart a way forward. If the department of defense could do nothing else, but unify a community and allow that community to provide a means for the exchange of ideas and independent thought, and provide these ideas to the younger members of that community, then the American cyber community would make a quantum leap forward. They could then let logic and reason guide the community, and, like our forefathers in aviation, design the campaign that would need a technological breakthrough to create a world-changing capability.

Once the American cyber community has developed an endstate, a vision, an organization, and a school, it must reorganize. There is a dilemma before the community, and while its members should be mentally flexible, they need their schools, doctrine, and planners to decide how much of our efforts should labor toward offensive vs. defensive means. Early airpower practitioners spent limited resources on offensive capabilities. They learned later, in World War II, that the bomber would not always get through and that the bomber needed defensive efforts, such as pursuit aircraft, to help protect it. The cyber community will make mistakes and not be any more successful at anticipating the future than its predecessors. But it must have a unified effort to plan for the future, a place where they can go "back to the drawing board", where the unwelcome, yet visionary beliefs of a future Claire Chennault can be praised and utilized, not cast aside. As the community reorganizes, toward an inevitably more offensive posture (inevitable as our present posture is completely defensive in nature) then they must influence the decision makers. The National Security, Defense, and Military Strategies are in need of reform.[142] Cyberspace does not exist to defend or protect, maintain the status quo or allow the use of the commons for traditional forces. Cyber warfare can attack, destroy, neutralize, and deter. Conventional wisdom says otherwise, but where could dissenting opinions thrive in a community with no unified organization, doctrine, or school?

The road ahead requires people. Not necessarily people that score the maximum on an physical fitness test or rifle qualification range, but the people who are the best at what they do. For the immediate future, the cyber community must recruit from wherever it can. Successful military organizations of the past indicate that the community must offer a career progression that rewards those who enter the organization early in their work experience, and can gain mastery over the course of their careers. It is unlikely the US government will recruit children, as do our competitors the Chinese, but it would be foolish to not recruit at all. To get the best and brightest we must examine how to recruit, where to recruit from, and what motivates the future American cyber warriors. Clearly, if the budget does not exist to recruit the best from the best American technical universities, then the cyber community will begin at a shortfall in our most precious commodity, the genius of the best we can recruit, motivate, and educate. The death of the Russian dam worker at the Sayano–Shushenskaya plant and the destruction of the nuclear centrifuges are among the first examples of the capabilities of this new type of warfare. They will not be the last. In these two specific instances, and many others in this paper, the megabyte got

---

[142] This refers to the 2010 National Security Strategy, 2008 National Defense Strategy, and 2011 National Military Strategy.

through. This new form of warfare is upon us, and it is our ability to adapt and take advantage of the changing nature of war that will determine our future success.

# BIBLIOGRAPHY

Alberts, David, John J. Garstka, and Frederick P. Stein. *Network Centric Warfare: Developing and Leveraging Information Superiority 2$^{nd}$ Edition.* Washington, DC: DoD C4ISR Cooperative Research Program, 1999.

Albright, David, Paul Brannan, and Christina Walrond. "Stuxnet Malware and Natanz: Update of ISIS December 22, 2010 Report." *Institute for Science and International Security,* February 15, 2011," http://isis-online.org/isis-reports/detail/stuxnet-malware-and-natanz-update-of-isis-december-22-2010-reportsupa-href1/ (accessed December 31, 2011).

Albright, David and Andrea Stricker. "ISIS Reports: Stuxnet Worm Targets Automated Systems for Frequency Converters: Are Iranian Centrifuges the Target?" *Institute for Science and International Security,* December 20, 2010," http://isis-online.org/isis-reports/detail/stuxnet-worm-targets-automated-systems-for-frequency-converters-is-irans-ce/8, (accessed December 31, 2011).

Ames, Roger T. trans. *Sun Tzu: The Art of Warfare.* NY: Ballantine, 1993.

Baldwin, Stanley. "The Bomber Will Always Get Through," (speech to the House of Commons, London, UK, November 10, 1932), posted by Brett Homan, Ph. D. on the Airminded Website, November 10, 2007, http://airminded.org/2007/11/10/the-bomber-will-always-get-through/ (accessed November 25, 2011).

Baocun, Wang. "The Current Revolution in Military Affair and its Impact on the Asia-Pacific Region," *China Military Science Review,* (136-142), April 2000.

Bergerud, Eric M. *Fire in the Sky: The Air War in the South Pacific.* Boulder, CO: Westview Press, 2000.

Bradley, Tony. "Zero Day Exploits," November 11, 2011. http://netsecurity.about.com/od/newsandeditorial1/a/aazeroday.htm (accessed April 3, 2012)

Boyko, Alexander and Sergey Popov. "Investigating the Sayano-Shushenskaya Hydro Power Plant Disaster," Power Magazine, December 1, 2010, http://www.powermag.com/issues/features/ Investigating- the-Sayano-Shushenskaya-Hydro-Power-Plant-Disaster_3229.html, (accessed April 3, 2012).

Boyd, Clark. "Cyber-war a Growing Threat Warn Experts." *BBC News.* June 17, 2010. http://www.bbc.co.uk/news/10339543 (accessed January 16, 2012).

Bright, Arthur. "Estonia Accuses Russia of 'Cyber Attack'". *The Christian Science Monitor.* May 17, 2007. http://www.csmonitor.com/2007/0517/p99s01-duts.html (accessed 14 January 2012).

Carr, Jeffrey. *Cyber Warfare: Mapping the Cyber Underworld.* Sebatopol, CA: O'Reilly Media, 2011.

Ceruzzi, Paul E. "The Challenge of Introducing History into a Computer Science Curriculum," 27-32, *Using History To Teach Computer Science and Related Disciplines.* Washington, DC: Computing Research Association, 2004.

Chairman, Joint Chiefs of Staff. *Joint Publication 3-0 2008: Joint Operations.* Washington, DC: Government Printing Office, 2008.

————. *The National Military Strategy of the United States of America, 2011: Redefining America's Military Leadership.* Washington, DC: Government Printing Office, 2011.

Corbett, Julian S., William Mitchell, David Jablonsky, A. T. Mahan, and Giulio Douhet. *Roots of Strategy: Book 4: 4 Military Classics.* Mechanicsburg, PA: Stackpole Books, 1999.

Craven, Wesley F. and James L. Cate. *The Army Air Forces in World War II.* Chicago: USAF Historical Division, 1948.

Danchev, Dancho. "Coordinated Russia vs Georgia Cyberattack." *ZDnet.* August 8, 2008. http://www.zdnet.com/blog/security/coordinated-russia-vs-georgia-cyber-attack-in-progress/1670 (accessed February 1, 2012).

Doughty, Robert A. *The Breaking Point: Sedan and the Fall of France, 1940.* Hamdon, CT: Archon, 1990.

Douhet, Giulio and Dino Ferrari. *The Command of the Air.* Washington, D.C.: Air Force History and Museums Program, 1998; 1942.

Evans, Martin Marix. *The Fall of France: Act with Daring.* Oxford, UK: Osprey Publishing, 2000.

The Express Tribune. "36 Government Sites Hacked by 'Indian Cyber Army'," *The Express Tribune Online*, November 30, 2010. http://tribune.com.pk/story/83967/36-government-websites-hacked-by-indian-cyber-army/ (accessed December 30, 2011.)

Fletcher, Owen. "China Denies Cyber Spy Network Charges," *PC World*, Mar 31, 2009, http://www.pcworld.com/article/162270/china_denies_cyber_spy_network_charges.html, (accessed January 1, 2012).

———. "China Takes Step to Toughen Hacking Laws," *Computerworld*, February 2, 2010. http://www.computerworld.com/s/article/9150718/China_takes_step_to_toughen _hacking_laws (accessed January 1, 2012).

Freedman, Lawrence. *Deterrence.* Cambridge, UK: Polity Press, 2004.

Fulghum, David A. and Douglas Barrie. "Israel Used Electronic Attack in Air strike Against Syrian Mystery Target," *Aviation Week & Space Technology*, (October 8, 2007), http://www.Aviationweek.com/aw/generic/story.jsp?channel=defense&id=news/aw 100807p2.xml&headline=Israel%20used%20electronic%20attack%20in%20air%20strike %20against%20Syrian%20mystery%20target&prev=10 (accessed January 10, 2012).

Gabbay, Tiffany. "Israeli Defense Forces Build Elite Hacker Team Amid Growing Cyber-Warfare Threat," (January 13, 2012), http://www.theblaze.com/stories/israeli-defense-forces-build-elite-hacker-team-amid-growing-cyber-warfare-threat/ (accessed January 13, 2012).

Greer, Thomas H. *The Development of Air Doctrine in the Army Air Arm, 1917-1941.* Washington, DC: Office of Air Force History, U.S. Air Force, 1985.

Griffith, Samuel B. ed. and trans. *Sun Tzu: The Art of War.* New York: Oxford University Press, 1971.

Hansell, Haywood S. *The Air Plan that Defeated Hitler.* Atlanta: Higgins-McArthur/Longino & Porter, 1979.

Headquarters, Department of the Army. *Field Manual 5-0 2010: The Operations Process.* Washington, DC: Government Printing Office, 2010.

———. *Field Manual 3-0 2008: Operations.* Washington, DC: Government Printing Office, 2008.

Henderson, Scott. *The Dark Visitor: Inside the World of Chinese Hackers.* Baltimore, MD: Henderson, 2007.

Higham, Robin D. and Stephen J. Harris, *Why Air Forces Fail: The Anatomy of Defeat.* Lexington, KY: University of Kentucky Press, 2006

Holley, Irving B. Jr., *Ideas and Weapons.* Ann Arbor, MI: University of Michigan, 1983.

Horne, Alistair. *To Lose a Battle: France 1940.* London, UK: Penguin Books, 1969.

Hurley, Alfred F. *Billy Mitchell: Crusader for Air Power.* Bloomington: Indiana University Press, 1975.

Janczewski, Lech and Andrew M. Colarik. *Cyber Warfare and Cyber Terrorism.* Hershey: Information Science Reference, 2008.

Johnson, David E. *Fast Tanks and Heavy Bombers: Innovation in the U.S. Army, 1917-1945.* Ithaca: Cornell University Press, 1998.

Johnson, Robert. "New Cyber Attacks Will Target Power Grids And Major Public Works," *Business Insider,* (March 10, 2012), http://articles.businessinsider.com/2011-09-14/news/30153012_1_data-theft-turbine-cyber-warfare (accessed February 2, 2012).

Keegan, John. *Intelligence in War Intelligence in War: The Value and Limitations of What the Military Can Learn About the Enemy.* New York: Vintage Books, 2002.

Keizer, Gregg. "Stuxnet Code Hints at Possible Israeli Origin," September 30, 2010. *Computer World.* http://www.computerworld.com/s/article/9188982/Stuxnet_code_hints _at_possible _Israeli_ origin_researchers_say (accessed April 3, 2012).

Kramer, Franklin D., Stuart H. Starr, Larry K. Wentz, and National Defense University. Center for Technology and National Security Policy. *Cyberpower and National Security.* Washington, DC: National Defense University Press, Potomac Books, 2009.

Krekel, Brian. "Capability of the People's Republic of China to Conduct Cyber Warfare and Computer Network Exploitation." Paper prepared for the U.S.-China Economic and Security Review Commission, Washington, DC, October 22, 2009. http://www.uscc.gov /researchpapers/2009/NorthropGrumman_PRC_ Cyber_ paper_FINAL_Approved%20 Report_16Oct2009.pdf (accessed December 28, 2011).

Krepinevich, Andrew F. "The Way to Respond to China," *The Los Angeles Times,* (November 9, 2011), http://articles.latimes.com/2011/nov/09/opinion/la-oe-krepinevich-pacific-20111109 (accessed April 3, 2012).

Kuhn, Thomas. *The Essential Tension: Selected Studies in Scientific Tradition and Change.* Chicago, University of Chicago Press, 1977.

Langner, Ralph. "Cracking Stuxnet: A 21st-Century Cyber Weapon," March, 2011. http://www.ted.com/talks/ralph_langner_cracking_stuxnet_a_21st_century_cyberweapon .html (accessed January 30, 2012).

Lewis, W. David. "Edward V. Rickenbacker's Reaction to Civil Aviation Policy in the 1930s: A Hidden Dimension." In *Reconsidering a Century of Flight,* edited by Roger D. Launius and Janet R. Daly Bedarek. Chapel Hill, NC: University of North Carolina Press, 2003.

Libicki, Martin C. *Conquest in Cyberspace: National Security and Information Warfare.* New York, NY: Cambridge University Press, 2007.

———. *Cyberdeterrence and Cyberwar.* Santa Monica, CA: Rand, 2009.

Liddell Hart, B. H. *Strategy, 2^nd Edition*, New York: Meridian, 1991.

Lidwell, William, Kritina Holden and Jill Butler. *Universal Principles of Design 11^th Edition.* Beverly, MA: Rockport Publishers, 2010.

MacIsaac, David. "Voices from the Central Blue: The Air Power Theorists." In *Makers of Modern Strategy from Machiavelli to the Nuclear Age*, edited by Peter Paret, 624-647. Princeton, NJ: Princeton University Press, 1986.

Mallet, Pascal. "AFP: Stuxnet Worm Brings Cyber Warfare Out of Virtual World." *Agence France-Presse*, (October 1, 2010), http://www.google.com/hostednews/afp/article /ALeq M5hWP5 Ga_K2k4oOosf Mz39JFifrDaQ?docId=CNG.0c3a53ff7267f11501 a5b3dbd9567dbf.2d1 (accessed 31 January 2012).

Markoff, John. "A Code for Chaos." *The New York Times*, (October 3, 2010), http://www.nytimes .com /2010/10/03/weekinreview/03markoff.html (accessed February 1, 2012).

———. *"Before the Gunfire, Cyberattacks." The New York Times*, (August 12, 2008). http://www.nytimes.com/2008/08/13/technology/13cyber.html (accessed January 31, 2012).

Markoff, John and David Barbosa, "Two China Schools Said to be Tied to Online Attacks." *The New York Times*. February 18, 2010. http://www.nytimes.com/2010/02/19/technology 19china.html, (accessed January 2, 2012).

Maurer, Maurer. *Aviation in the U.S. Army, 1919-1939.* Washington, DC: United States Air Force Historical Research Center, 1987.

Mosier, John. *The Blitzkrieg Myth: How Hitler and the Allies Misread the Strategic Realities of World War II.* New York: Harper Collins Publishers, 2003.

Murray, Williamson and Allan R. Millett, *Military Innovation in the Interwar Period.* Cambridge, UK: Cambridge University Press, 1996.

Murphy, Matt. "War in the Fifth Domain. Are the Mouse and Keyboard the New Weapons of Conflict?" *The Economist*, (July 1, 2010), http://www.economist.com/node/16478792 (accessed January 21, 2012).

Murray, Williamson and Allan R. Millett, *Military Innovation in the Interwar Period*. Cambridge, UK: Cambridge University Press, 1996.

O'Connell, Robert L. *Of Arms and Men: A History of War, Weapons, and Aggression.* New York: Oxford University Press, 1989.

Osgood, Kenneth A. *Total Cold War: Eisenhower's Secret Propaganda Battle at Home and Abroad.* Lawrence: University of Kansas, 2006.

Overy, Richard. *Why the Allies Won.* New York: W. W. Norton & Company, 1995.

Pakistan Defence Website. "Top Ten Weapons of Pakistan," http://www.defence.pk/forums /pakistan-strategic-forces/127546-top-10-future-weapons-pakistan-3.html (accessed February 3, 2012).

Pape, Robert A. *Bombing to Win: Air Power and Coercion in War.* Ithaca, NY: Cornell University Press, 1996.

The People's Republic of China, Information Office of the State Council. *China's National Defense in 2008.* Beijing, http://www.china.org.cn/ government/ whitepaper/ node_7060059.htm (accessed January 12, 2012).

Pik-kwan Chan, Vivien "HK: SCMP Report on PRC Officials Condemning Hacker Attacks," *Hong Kong South China Morning Post*, May 8 , 2001.

President, United States of America. *The National Security Strategy, May 2010.* (Washington, DC: Government Printing Office, 2010

Rattray, Gregory J. *Strategic Warfare in Cyberspace.* Cambridge, MA.: MIT Press, 2001.

Republic of Georgia, "Russian Invasion of Georgia," www.georgiaupdate.gov.ge (accessed December 24, 2011).

Sageman, Marc. *Leaderless Jihad: Terror Networks in the Twenty-first Century.* Philadelphia: University of Pennsylvania Press, 2008.

————. *Understanding Terror Networks.* Philadelphia: University of Pennsylvania Press, 2004.

Schmidle, Robert E. LtGen, USMC, Deputy Commander USCYBERCOM. "USMC Cyberspace Update," Presentation, meeting of the AFCEA Quantico-Potomac Chapter, Quantico, VA, March 31, 2011

Shen Yongjun and Su Ruozhou, "PLA Sets to Push Forward Informationalization Drive from Three Aspects," *PLA Daily Online*, (January 11, 2006), http://english.chinamil.com.cn/site2/news-channels/2006-01/11/content_382378.htm (accessed December 31, 2011).

Sherry, Michael S. *The Rise of American Air Power: The Creation of Armageddon.* New Haven, CT: Yale University Press, 1989.

Slater, Robert. *Jack Welch and the GE Way: Management Insights and Leadership Secrets of the Legendary CEO.* New York: McGraw-Hill. 1999.

Smith, David J. and Khatuna Mshvisobadze, "Russia, Georgia and the Shape of Cyber Wars to Come." Presentation, SMi Cyber Security Forum Initiative, Istanbul, May 16, 2011.

Sokolski, Henry D. *Getting MAD: Nuclear mutual assured destruction, its origins and practice.* Carlisle Barracks, PA: Strategic Studies Institute, U.S. Army War College, 2004.

————. *Nuclear Power's Global Expansion: Weighing its Costs and Risks.* Carlisle, PA: Strategic Studies Institute, U.S. Army War College, 2010.

————. *Taming the Next Set of Strategic Weapons Threats.* Carlisle Barracks, PA: Strategic Studies Institute, U.S. Army War College, 2006.

Sweetman, John, David Coward and Gary Johnstone, *The Dambusters.* London: Time Warner Books, 2003.

Stiennon, Richard. *Surviving Cyberwar.* Plymouth, UK: Government Institutes, 2010.

Szayna, Thomas S. et al. *The Emergence of Peer Competitors: A Framework for Analysis.* Washington, DC: The Rand Arroyo Center, 2001.

Tate, James P. *The Army and Its Air Corps: Army Policy toward Aviation, 1919-1941.* Washington, DC: Government Printing Office, 1998.

Thomas, Timothy L. "China's Electronic Strategies," *Military Review*, May-June 2001.

Thurston, David B. *The World's Most Significant and Magnificent Aircraft: Evolution of the Modern Airplane.* Warrendale, PA: Society of Automotive Engineers, 2000.

Trest, Warren A. *Air Force Roles and Missions: A History*, Washington, DC: Air Force History and Museums Program, 1998.

Tuchman, Barbara W. *The Guns of August*, New York: Ballantine Books, 1962.

U.S. Army Training and Doctrine Command, Joint and Army Concepts Division. *United States Army Concepts, 2015-2024.* Fort Monroe, VA: Government Printing Office, 2007.

U.S. Department of Defense. "*Quadrennial Defense Review February 2010,*" (February 12, 2010), www.defense.gov/qdr/images/QDR_as_of_12Feb10_1000.pdf (accessed October 13, 2011).

Ventre, Daniel. *Information Warfare,* London: ISTE Ltd, 2009.

Wolk, Herman S. *Toward Independence The Emergence of the U.S. Air Force, 1945-1947.* Washington, DC: Air Force History and Museums Program, 1996.

Zetter, Kim. "Clues Suggest Stuxnet Virus Was Built for Subtle Nuclear Sabotage," *Wired,* November 15, 2010. http://www.wired.com/threatlevel/2010/11/stuxnet-clues/ (accessed December 31, 2011).

———. "Google Hack Attack Was Ultra Sophisticated, New Details Show." *Wired.* January 14, 2010. http://www.wired.com/threatlevel/2010/01/operation-aurora/ (accessed December 30, 2011).

———. "Google to Stop Censoring Search Results in China After Hack Attack," *Wired,* January 12, 2010. http://www.wired.com/threatlevel/2010/01/google-censorship-china/, (accessed December 30, 2011).

———. "How Digital Detectives Deciphered Stuxnet," *Wired,* July 11, 2011. http://www.wired.com /threatlevel/2011/07/how-digital-detectives-deciphered-stuxnet/2/ (accessed December 27, 2011).